365 Food

Kids Love To Eat

By Sheila Ellison and Judith Gray

Forward March™Press
Carson City, NV

Published By:
Forward March, Inc.
2701 Conestoga Dr., Suite 121
Carson City, NV 89706

First Printing, Aug. 1989
Seventh Printing, June 1993

ISBN# 0-9620467-5-2

U.S. Booksellers Distributor: Publishers Group West 1-800-788-3123

Cover drawing by: Jay Ritchey

Printed in the United States of America

To the
wonderful
healthy kids
with whom I
have shared
food shopping,
cooking,
mealtimes,
and cleaning up . . .

Jonathan

Andrew

Kirsty

Riki

— Judith

To my husband Riki,
our children
Wesley, Brooke
and Rhett.
For being my
creative
inspiration!
To my brothers
and sisters:
Susan, Karen
David, Brian
and Brennan
who have shared
mealtimes and memories.

— Sheila

Introduction by the Authors

Families spend considerable time and energy on preparing food, putting it on the table, and supervising its consumption. Eating, especially for children, is a very important activity and one which enables them to develop social skills, communication skills, and self-esteem. Mealtimes, moreover are opportunities for family bonding, sharing, interaction, relaxation, and learning consideration of others.

After many years of cooking for children and families, it occurred to us that today's parents needed a practical, comprehensive, easy to follow cookbook designed with kid's palates and appetites in mind. As our title suggests, our goal is to provide a sufficient range and variety of recipes so that you will be able to serve foods that your child will like and try.

We hope you will use this book when you are planning menus or when you are looking for recipes which balance or complement your meals or other food events. To that end we have included a sensible array of food sections, including snacks, fruits, salads, soups, breakfasts, and foods for when you and your family are on the go. Other sections focus on do-it-yourself ideas for kids, foreign dishes, sick days, holidays, and children's parties.

In order to better acquaint you with the job of feeding children, we have carefully included some special items. You will find a section on healthful food substitutions and suggestions plus another one on table management ideas and recommendations. We feel that parents not only need good recipe books, but that they also need guidelines for encouraging healthy attitudes towards food and lifelong wholesome eating habits. The poems that begin each section were written by Shari Cohen, writer of children's self-help and poetry books. They are delightful and humorous and we hope you will share them with your children. Finally, we have included a comprehensive index for quick access to the recipes.

All our recipes have been kitchen-tested, child-tested, and professionally reviewed for nutritional content. However, we feel that we must remind you that some items are potentially dangerous in the hands and mouths of small children. These are whole nuts, popcorn, seeds, and toothpicks. Also, where milk is used, please substitute with non-fat, low-fat or soy-based milks at your discretion.

As you use and enjoy our book we want you to know that we would gratefully appreciate your suggestions and comments. We wish you and your family good eating and good health.

Sheila Ellison   Judith Gray

Table Management for Families

O All family members should wash and dry hands before eating

O Children should not be forced to eat what they don't want

O Children should refuse food tactfully and politely

O If a food is not on the table, then it is not available

O When serving your child's food, make sure the portions are small. . . she can always ask for seconds

O The smaller the child, the slower he eats

O Always have bread or rolls on the table

O Instruct children to wipe their hands on a napkin, not on their clothes

O Wait until **everyone** is seated before anyone commences eating

O People bring food up to their mouths and animals take their mouths down to their food

O Children can be temporarity excused from the table for nose blowing, coughing or to go to the bathroom

- O Adults at the table should avoid monopolising the conversation
- O Parents are the chief role models for children when it comes to manners and eating
- O Establish regular mealtimes
- O Establish times for snacks too
- O Children should come to the table reasonably hungry
- O Ban the following expressions - "Yuk!", "Do I *have* to eat this?", "Gross!", and "What *is* this?"
- O NO gum chewing at the table
- O Adults should not use mealtime to discuss matters that only concern them
- O Make an attempt to have something on the table that your child likes
- O Allow children to select the food they want from the table
- O Be considerate of everyone else at the table
- O Make sure that family eating is enjoyable and eagerly anticipated by all

Healthful Suggestions

- Trim fats from meats and poultry before cooking
- The yolk of an egg contains all the fat. Try using one egg yolk with 2 or more egg whites
- Replace ground beef wherever possible with lean ground turkey
- Buy products made naturally: peanut butter, preserves, mayonnaise, and ketchup
- Pure maple syrup is an excellent substitute for sugar
- Spend some time reading labels and looking for pure foods and all natural ingredients
- Whole-grain breads, cereals, flours, and baking mixes are important: they have more fiber
- Avoid using baking powder that contains aluminum
- Use canned skim milk in sauces, soups, and other recipes that call for cream
- Most children love peanut butter - try other natural nut butters for variety
- Canola oil is a great healthful vegetable oil: it is suitable for any recipe
- For good protein sources try peas, beans, lentils, nuts, and seeds
- Instead of fruit-flavored yogurts use plain yogurt and add fresh fruit or natural preserves
- Ice milk is a good substitute for ice cream; but sherbert is even better
- To reduce your family's salt intake, chose herbs, spices, garlic, or lemon as alternatives
- Shop for fruits frozen without sugar or canned in natural juice or water: check the labels
- If you would like your family to eat more healthfully, start changing foods very gradually: a slow switch is better than no switch!

Healthful Substitutions

1 teaspoon baking powder *equals* 1/2 teaspoon each cream of tartar and baking soda

1 square baking chocolate *equals* 3 tablespoons cocoa plus 1 tablespoon butter **or** 3 tablespoons carob plus 2 tablespoons water

1 cup sugar *equals* 3/4 cup honey **or** 1 1/4 cups molasses **or** 3/4 cup pure maple syrup

1 cup white flour *equals* 3/4 cup whole-wheat flour **or** 3/4 cup graham flour **or** 1 cup whole-wheat pastry flour

1 cup butter *equals* 1 cup margarine **or** 7/8 cup vegetable oil

1 cup buttermilk *equals* 1 cup milk plus 1 3/4 tablespoons cream of tartar

2 eggs *equal* 1 egg plus 2 egg whites **or** 2 tablespoons oil plus 1 tablespoon water

1 cup milk *equals* 1/2 cup evaporated milk plus 1/2 cup water **or** 3 tablespoons powdered milk plus 1 cup water

1 cup sour cream *equals* 1 tablespoon lemon juice **or** vinegar and 1 cup evaporated milk **or** 1 cup plain yogurt **or** 1 cup buttermilk

1 cup whipped cream *equals* 1 cup non-fat milk powder whipped with 1 cup ice water

1 cup whipped cream = 1 4 ounce (125g) package non-dairy whipped topping
= 1 cup non-fat milk powder whipped with 1 cup ice water

SNACK   BROCCOLI 'n CHERRY TOMATOES SautED sprinkle of cheese

Table of Contents

Beverages

Red and purple berries
Ice cubes that are pink
Swirls of green whipped cream
Mixed up in this drink.

Blended thick and frosty
Best served with a lunch
How I love my recipe
for "ROBIN'S RAINBOW PUNCH!"

Cranana Crush

Ingredients
1 small banana, sliced
1 cup cranberry juice
1/3 cup orange juice
5 ice cubes

Directions
In a blender or food processor, combine the banana, cranberry juice, orange juice and ice. Cover and process till smooth. Drink! Yield: 2 to 3 servings.

Note: In <u>The Practical Parent</u>, the authors Genevieve Painter and Raymond Corsini believe that it is morally wrong for one member of the family to do less than his or her 'fair share' . It is equally wrong, they say, for a family member to do more than his or her share of the chores. No member should be, in effect, the other's servant. (New York: Simon & Schuster, 1984), p. 99. In other words, family chores should be equitably shared amongst all.

Watermelon Whirl

Summer

Ingredients
1 cup watermelon chunks, seeded and chilled
1/4 cup unsweetened red grape juice
1 scoop plain ice cream
1/2 cup crushed ice
1 or 2 drops natural red food coloring

Directions
Place watermelon, grape juice, and ice cream in a blender
jar and process until smooth and thick. Place the crushed
ice in a tall glass. Pour the blender mixture over the ice.
Gently stir in the food color. Use a pink or white straw and serve.
Yield: 2 servings.

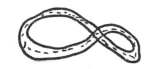

*Note: Children need firm limits. Setting limits is a gift of love.
Limits are the foundation of security. Kids who are lucky enough to
have limits placed upon them in loving ways are secure enough to
build self confidence and are less likely to act up or misbehave.*

2

Chocolate Frosted Shake

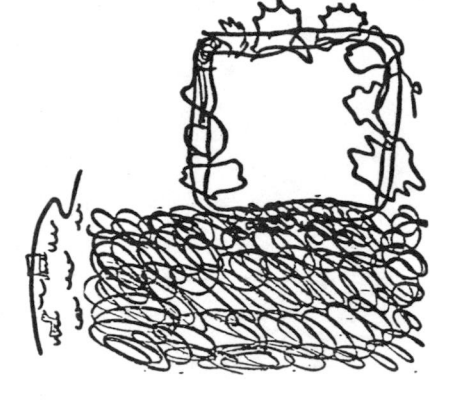

Ingredients
1 cup lowfat milk
1 scoop chocolate ice cream
1 tablespoon chocolate syrup

Directions
Put all ingredients in a blender.
Process until thick and smooth.
Pour into tall glass. Yield: 1 tall glass.

Note: *Keep a record of your child's growth. Attach a yard (1 meter) rule or a dressmaker's tape measure to the doorway of the kitchen or bathroom. With a felt pen, regularly mark your child's height onto the measure and add the date. Children like to be compared with older siblings so use a different color for each family member.*

3

Cranberry Tea

Ingredients
4 cups cranberries
2 sticks cinnamon
3 cups prepared frozen orange juice
2 teaspoons lemon juice
1 1/2 cups sugar

Directions
Place cranberries in a saucepan and cover with water. Put in the cinnamon sticks and boil gently until berries are soft. Remove the cinnamon sticks. Strain the berries through a colander, crushing slightly. Add the prepared orange juice, lemon juice, and sugar. Stir until sugar is dissolved. Add more water to make a gallon (2 liters). Simmer for 15 minutes. Serve hot in a mug or cup over a slice of lemon. Yield: 8 servings.

Note: *In case cranberries are out of season, 1 bottle of cranberry juice makes the equivalent of 4 cups of berries. Reduce the sugar considerably when using bottled or frozen juice.*

4

Fruit Pudding Nog

Ingredients
1 envelope vanilla pudding mix
2 cups milk
1 cup water
2 eggs, separated
1 cup fruit juice - orange, grape or apple.
1/4 teaspoon grated nutmeg

Directions
Place pudding, milk, water, and egg yolks in a saucepan and beat with a wire whisk. Place over a low heat, stirring constantly, until thickened, about 15 minutes. Remove from heat and cool. Meanwhile, beat egg whites until stiff. Add fruit juice to pudding mixture and blend. Gradually pour pudding into egg whites. Stir until just mixed. Ladle into glasses and sprinkle nutmeg on top. Enjoy with a parfait spoon. Yield: 4 - 6 servings.

Note: *Pudding can be prepared in the microwave. It will thicken in 5 to 6 minutes. If using no-cook pudding mix, omit egg yolks and do not heat.*

Maple Ice Milk

Ingredients
1 cup maple syrup
1 egg, beaten
1 cup ice water
1 cup instant milk powder

Directions
Chill beaters and a mixing bowl in the refrigerator. Heat the maple syrup over a double boiler. Add to the beaten egg and then return mixture to double boiler. Cook for 15 minutes stirring constantly until mixture thickens. Set aside to cool. Beat milk powder and ice water in chilled bowl with chilled beaters until stiff. Fold in the maple syrup mixture and blend well. Return to the freezer and chill, stirring occasionally. Before hardening, scoop into glasses and serve with a spoon. Yield: 4 - 6 servings

Note: It is harder and takes longer to beat powdered milk into a stiff consistency than cream. Chilled bowl and beaters are a must.

6

Tootie Fruitie Smoothie

Ingredients

1 ripe banana, peeled and sliced
6 fresh or frozen strawberries
1 cup unflavored yogurt
1/2 cup fruit sherbert

Directions

Put all ingredients into a blender.
Whirl until smooth. Serve in tall
glasses and garnish with a slice of
fruit or ground nutmeg. Yield: 1 large
serving.

Vanilla yogurt
flavored yogurt
strawberries
sugar
milk

Note: *Every child seeks a self-picture of herself as capable and
strong. And behavior matches self-image. Dorothy Corkille Briggs in
Your Child's Self Esteem (New York: Doubleday, 1975), adds that
even the way a child speaks is colored by her feelings about herself.
(p. 22)*

7

Willie Winkies' Hot Cocoa Nightcap

Ingredients
1 teaspoon cocoa powder
1 teaspoon sugar
1 cup milk
Few drops vanilla extract

Directions
Put cocoa, sugar, and 1 tablespoon milk in a cup and stir until smooth and shiny. Gradually pour in remaining milk. Heat in microwave oven for 2 minutes or until hot, but not boiling. Add vanilla, stir, and enjoy. Hot cocoa can also be prepared in a small saucepan. Be sure to stir constantly while heating milk. Serve with a cookie or graham cracker before bed. . . but remember to brush teeth! Yield: 1 serving.

Note: *A warm drink before bed is said to promote sleepiness and relaxation. By the end of the day, most children welcome some quiet time and a bedtime story.*

Strawberry Fizz

Ingredients
1 cup frozen strawberries
1/2 cup low-fat milk
1 can diet strawberry soda

Directions
Place all ingredients in a blender and blend until smooth. Pour into glasses and serve immediately. Other soda flavors can be used instead of strawberry for a fruity taste.

Note: It is the child's feeling about being loved or unloved that affects how he will develop, says Dorothy Corkille Briggs in her book *Your Child's Self Esteem* (New York: Doubleday, 1975), p. 4. A loved child feels secure and cherished with the result that he or she will develop a healthy self-esteem.

9

Apple Zinger

Ingredients
1 cup natural apple juice
1 cup water
10 cinnamon red hots
5 whole cloves

Directions
Heat the ingredients until the red hot candies dissolve. Simmer for 5 minutes. Strain and serve warm or cold.
Yield: 2 servings.

Note: Did you know that the apple tree belongs to the rose family of plants? Crab apples of course, look a lot like rose hips, the fruit of roses, and can be used to make fruit juices and 'rosehip syrup' found on page 309.

10

Summer Lemonade

Ingredients
3 lemons
1/2 cup sugar
1 cup hot water
4 cups cold water
Ice cubes
Fresh mint leaves

Directions
Cut lemons in half and squeeze the juice out of all except 1 half. Put the juice and the sugar into a tall pitcher. Add one cup of hot water and stir until the sugar is dissolved. Add the rest of the water and stir. Add some ice cubes. Cut the lemon half into slices. Rinse off the mint leaves. Pour into glasses and garnish with lemon slices or mint leaves. Yield: 4 servings.

Note: This drink is a much healthier alternative to store-bought packets of lemonade mix. For pink lemonade, add a drop of red food coloring and garnish with sliced strawberries.

11

Simple Egg Nog

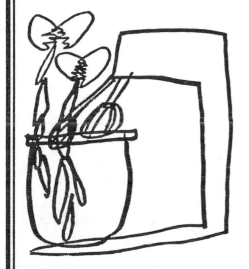

Ingredients
2 eggs
1/4 cup honey
Pinch of salt
4 cups cold milk
1 teaspoon vanilla extract
Natural yellow food coloring

Directions
Beat or blend the first 4 ingredients until smooth.
Add the vanilla and one drop of food coloring. Keep
in the refrigerator until ready to drink. Can be
heated slowly and served warm when it's cold
outside. Yield: 4 servings.

12

Sherbert Party Punch

Ingredients

4 cups fruit juice
2 cups soda water
1 pint (500ml) frozen sherbert
Fruit garnishes

Directions

Mix together fruit juice and soda water in a punch bowl. Carefully place the sherbert in the bowl and stir until partially melted. Ladle punch into glasses and garnish with strawberries, orange slices, cherries, or pineapple chunks. Yield: 8 servings.

Note: *In their book* The Practical Parent, *(New York: Simon & Schuster, 1984) Genevieve painter and Raymond Corsini state that a child should not be expected to eat the same amount or even the same foods, at each meal. Somedays a child will eat large amounts of food, and other days only a little. And that's OK.*

13

Yogurt Banana Shake

Ingredients

8 ounces (250g) low-fat yogurt - any flavor
1 ripe banana
1 cup milk
Ground nutmeg

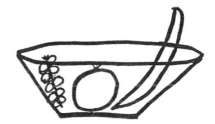

Directions

Peel banana and break into small pieces. Drop into a blender and add yogurt and milk. Blend until smooth and thick, about 1 minute. Pour into 2 small glasses or 1 tall one. Sprinkle nutmeg on top before serving. Yield: 1 shake.

Note: *Yogurt is an ancient drink prepared from milk curdled by bacteria. In India for instance, fresh yogurt is made daily by saving a little of the drink, adding milk and letting it sit in a warm place overnight while it thickens and sours. It is an excellent substitute for sour cream.*

14

Sun Tea

Ingredients
3 tea bags, caffeine-free teas are best
1 gallon glass jar
Flavorings
- bruised mint leaves
- thin lemon slices
- cinnamon stick
- cloves
Sugar or honey to taste

Directions
Fill the jar with cold water. Drop in the teabags, keeping the strings on the outside. Cover opening. Let jar sit in the sun for 4 hours. Remove teabags and add a flavoring. Chill. Serve over ice cubes and sweeten to taste. Yield: 16 servings.

Note: *Tea is an ancient drink originating in China. Iced tea was introduced to America in 1904 at the St Louis World's Fair.*

Breads and Muffins

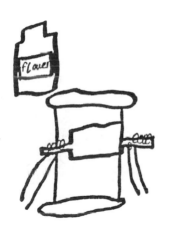

Ripe bananas squished in honey
melted butter, soft and runny
Watch her with a silly grin
dribbling batter tin to tin
lumpy muffins in the pan
created by our baby, Jan.

Plump Pear Bread

Ingredients

2 cups whole-wheat flour
2 teaspoons baking powder
1 cup diced fresh pears
1/4 cup pear or apple juice
1/2 cup mild honey
1/3 cup mayonnaise
1 egg
1/2 teaspoon vanilla

Directions

Preheat oven to 350°F (180°C). Combine the first two ingredients
in bowl. Place remaining ingredients in the blender and blend
until smooth. Pour over dry ingredients and mix just until blended.
Pour into two greased 8x4x3 inch loaf pans. Bake 50-60 minutes.
Yield: 16 servings.

16

Magical Cinnamon Rolls

Ingredients
1 package of frozen bread dough
1 tablespoon butter or margarine
1/2 cup brown sugar
2 teaspoons cinnamon
1/2 cup raisins, optional

Directions
Thaw dough to room temperature. Pat dough into a rectangle.
Spread with the melted butter. Combine the sugar and cinnamon
and sprinkle over butter. Evenly distribute raisins over top.
Starting with longer side, roll up. Seal edges tightly. With a sharp
knife, cut roll into 1 inch (20 cm) pieces. Place rolls on greased
cookie sheet, allowing room to spread, and let rise in a warm
place until light and doubled in size. Bake at 375°F (190°C) for 20
minutes. Remove from oven and while still warm drizzle with frosting mix or a honey glaze. Yield: 24 rolls.

17

Zucchini Bread

Ingredients
1 1/2 cups unbleached flour
1 1/2 teaspoons baking soda
1/4 teaspoon cinnamon
2 eggs, beaten
1/2 cup sugar
1/2 cup vegetable oil
1 teaspoon vanilla
Pinch of salt
1 1/2 cups unpeeled grated zucchini

Directions
Preheat oven to 350°F (180°C). Sift together the flour, baking soda, and cinnamon. Add the eggs, sugar, oil, vanilla, and a pinch of salt. Stir until just moistened. Quickly fold in the grated zucchini. Pour mixture into a greased and floured loaf pan. Bake for 1 hour or until a straw comes out clean. Cool for 10 minutes before turning out onto a wire rack. If desired, 1 cup ground pecans can be added along with the zucchini. Yield: 1 loaf.

18

Very Berry Muffins

Directions

Preheat oven to 400°F (200°C). Sift all dry ingredients together except topping. Add berries and mix until well coated. In a small bowl, beat eggs well and add melted butter and milk. Quickly stir liquid mixture into dry mix. Stir until just blended. Fill muffin cups 3/4 full. Sprinkle a teaspoon of cinnamon sugar on top of each muffin. Bake for 20 minutes or until a toothpick tests clean. Yield: 24.

Note: Suggestions for berries - cranberries, blueberries, black currants, raspberries, pitted cherries, and loganberries.

Ingredients

2　cups flour
3　teaspoons baking powder
1/2　cup sugar
1/4　teaspoon salt
1　cup fresh or frozen berries
2　eggs
1/2　cup melted butter
1　cup milk
Cinnamon sugar for topping

19

Date Scones

Ingredients

2 cups unbleached flour
2 rounded teaspoons baking powder
Pinch salt
2 ounces (50g) butter or margarine
3/4 cup milk
8 ounces (500g) pitted dates

Directions

Preheat oven to 400°F (200°C). Sift dry ingredients into a medium bowl. Cut or rub margarine into the flour mixture. Chop the dates and add. Make a hole in the middle of the mixture and pour in milk. Quickly stir until a soft dough forms. Turn out onto a floured surface and knead into a rectangle, 12 x 9 inches. Roll or pat to 1/2 inch thickness. Cut into 12 to 16 squares and place close together on a greased cookie tray. Bake for 10 to 12 minutes. Yield: 12 - 16 scones.

20

Best Banana Bread

Ingredients

1 3/4 cups unbleached flour, sifted
2 1/4 teaspoons baking powder
1/4 teaspoon salt
1/3 cup margarine or butter

2/3 cup sugar
3/4 teaspoon grated lemon rind
3 or 4 ripe bananas, pulped
1 or 2 beaten eggs

Directions

Preheat oven to 350°F (180°C). Sift together the dry ingredients and set aside. Blend margarine, sugar, and lemon rind until creamy. Add the beaten eggs and banana pulp and stir until thoroughly mixed in. Add the dry ingredients in 3 parts and blend until smooth. Dollop the batter into a greased and floured loaf pan. Bake in the center of the oven about 45 to 50 minutes. Test with a toothpick or straw. Do not overcook. Cool before slicing. Yield: 1 loaf.

Note: *Young food tastes need shaping. Dr Story of the University of Minnesota School of Public Health suggests offering children as many nutritious choices as possible, serving sweets sometimes but* **never as rewards or bribes.** *Children* **can** *learn to eat well.*

21

Zucchini Bran Muffins

Ingredients

2 cups bran cereal
1 cup shredded zucchini
3/4 cup milk
1 egg
1/2 cup sugar
1/3 cup vegetable oil
1 1/2 cups unbleached flour
2 teaspoons baking powder
1/2 teaspoon each ginger and cinnamon

Directions

Preheat the oven to 375°F (190°C). In a large bowl mix together bran cereal, zucchini, milk, egg, oil, and sugar. Set aside. Sift together flour, baking powder, and spices and then add to bran mixture. Stir until just moistened. Drop batter into 12 well-greased muffin pans about 3/4 full. Bake for 30 minutes or until muffins are brown on top and firm to the touch. Serve warm or cool on wire rack. These muffins can be wrapped in airtight plastic wrap and frozen. Serve with butter or cream cheese. Yield: 24 muffins.

22

Hansel and Gretel Gingerbread

Ingredients

2 1/2 cups unbleached flour
2 teaspoons baking soda
1 teaspoon cinnamon
1 teaspoon ginger
1 teaspoon mixed spice

1 teaspoon cocoa
1 cup milk
1/2 cup light molasses
1/2 cup sugar
1/2 cup butter or margarine

Directions

Preheat oven to 350°F (180°C). Sift together all the dry ingredients in a large bowl. In a small saucepan or in the microwave oven, warm the milk, molasses, sugar and butter until blended, stirring frequently. Cool slightly then add to dry ingredients. Stir until blended, but do not over-stir. Pour into a greased and floured loaf pan. Bake for 40 minutes or until straw comes out clean. Yield: 1 loaf.

Note: *Encourage your children to brush and floss their teeth promptly after each meal. If that is not always possible, have them eat an apple or chew a sprig of parsley. The apples helps remove food particles and the parsley freshens the breath.*

23

Corny Corn Muffins

Ingredients

1 cup cornmeal
1 cup unbleached flour
2 teaspoons baking powder
1 tablespoon sugar
1 egg, beaten
1 cup milk
1/4 cup vegetable oil
Small can of corn, drained

Directions

Preheat oven to 425°F (220°C). Sift all the dry ingredients together into a medium bowl and set aside. Add the milk and oil to the beaten egg. Stir this mixture into the dry ingredients and add the corn. Do not over stir. Heat the muffin pans. Drop a little butter into each pan. Spoon into pans, 3/4 full. Bake 15 - 20 minutes. Yield: 24 muffins.

Note: *Cornbread mixes can be used to make these muffins. Remember however, that they contain a lot more sugar.*

24

Cinderella's Pumpkin Bread

Ingredients

1 cup cooked or canned pumpkin
1/2 cup vegetable oil
2 eggs, beaten
1/2 cup brown sugar
1/2 cup white sugar
2 cups unbleached flour, sifted

1 teaspoon baking soda
1/2 teaspoon each nutmeg and cinnamon
1 cup raisins
1/4 cup water

Directions

Preheat oven to 350°F (180°C). Beat together the eggs, oil, pumpkin, and sugars. Sift together the dry ingredients and add to pumpkin mixture. Stir in raisins and water. Pour into a greased and floured loaf pan. Bake for 1 hour or until straw comes out clean. Wait 10 minutes before turning out onto wire rack to cool. Yield: 1 loaf.

25

Savory Cheese Muffins

Ingredients

1 1/4 cups unbleached flour
3/4 cup whole-wheat flour
3 tablespoons grated parmesan cheese
3 tablespoons grated romano cheese
2 teaspoons baking powder
3/4 teaspoon dill weed

Pinch salt
1/8 teaspoon garlic powder
1 cup milk
1/4 cup vegetable oil
1 egg, beaten

Directions

Preheat oven to 400°F (200°C). In a bowl, combine flours, cheeses, baking powder, dill weed, salt, and garlic powder. Make a hole in the middle and add milk, oil, and egg. Stir just until dry ingredients are moistened. Spoon batter into baking cups, filling 3/4 full. Bake 18 to 20 minutes or until golden brown. If desired, during last 3 minutes top each muffin with a teaspoon of grated cheddar cheese. Yield: 20 muffins.

Note: *Paper baking cups can be used in conventional or micro-wave ovens. Use a double layer of cups when microwaving. Foil cups are generally easier to remove after baking than paper cups.*

26

Oatmeal Raisin Bread

Ingredients

2 packets active dry yeast
1/2 cup milk
1 cup cold water

1/4 cup butter or margarine
1/4 cup honey
1 cup raisins

2 cups uncooked oats
6 to 6 1/2 cups bread flour
2 teaspoons salt

Directions

Dissolve yeast in 1/4 cup warm water. Combine milk and cold water and heat until almost boiling. Pour hot liquid over butter, honey, raisins and salt in a large bowl and stir until butter melts. Cool to lukewarm. Add the yeast mixture and oats. Beat in 2 cups of the flour until mixture is smooth. Add the remaining flour and stir to make a soft dough. Turn out onto a lightly floured surface and knead until elastic, about 10 minutes. Place in a greased bowl, turn to coat and let stand covered until double in size. Punch dough down and shape to form 2 loaves. Place in greased loaf pans. Cover and let rise until nearly double. Bake at 375°F (190°C) for 45 minutes or until bread sounds hollow when tapped. Cool on racks. Yield: 2 loaves.

27

Leprechaun Soda Bread

Ingredients

4 cups unbleached flour
1/2 cup sugar
1 teaspoon baking soda
2 teaspoons baking powder
1/2 teaspoon salt

1/2 cup butter or margarine
1 cup currants or raisins
1 tablespoon caraway seed (optional)
1 egg
1 1/2 cups buttermilk or plain yogurt

Directions

Preheat oven to 375°F (190°C). Sift dry ingredients into a large bowl. Cut in butter with a pastry blender until mixture is crumbly. Stir in currants and caraway seeds. Combine egg and buttermilk in another bowl. Make hole in center of flour mixture and pour in liquid. Stir quickly to form a soft dough. Turn out onto a lightly floured board and shape into one large round loaf or 2 small ones. With a floured knife, cut into wedges but don't separate. Place loaves onto a greased cookie tray and bake for 45 minutes or until center is done. Remove from oven and cool on wire rack. Break open wedges and serve with butter if desired. Soda bread is best eaten the same day, but can be toasted for breakfast for up to 3 days. Yield: 12 - 16 servings.

28

Lazy Daisy Loaf

Ingredients

2 eggs
1 cup sugar
1 tablespoon melted butter
1 cup flour

1 teaspoon baking powder
Pinch of salt
1/2 cup milk
1 teaspoon vanilla extract

Directions

Preheat oven to 350°F (180°C). Beat the eggs and sugar until thick and stir in the melted butter. Sift together the flour, baking powder and salt. Alternate adding the dry ingredients with the milk. Lastly add the vanilla extract. Stir until blended. Grease and flour a loaf pan. Pour in the mixture and bake 35 to 40 minutes or until a straw comes out clean. Top with

Glaze:

In a small saucepan combine 1 1/2 tablespoons butter, 1/4 cup brown sugar, 1 tablespoon milk, and 1/2 cup unsweetened dessicated coconut. Cook for 5 - 7 minutes stirring constantly. Put glaze on loaf while it is still warm. Cool before slicing. Yield: 1 loaf.

29

Confetti Corn Bread

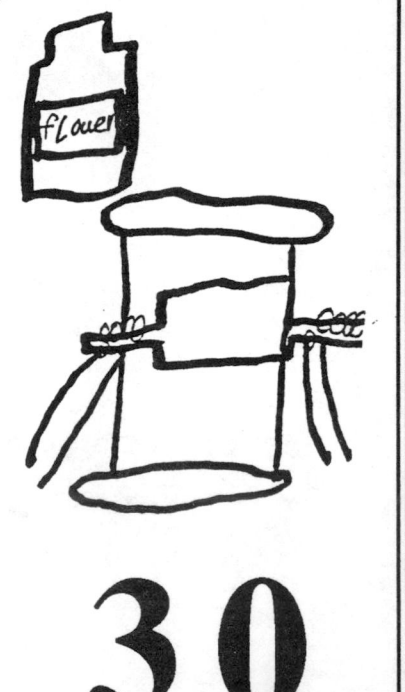

Ingredients

3/4 cups flour
1 cup cornmeal
2 tablespoons sugar
2 teaspoons baking powder
1/2 teaspoon baking soda
1/2 teaspoon salt

1/4 cup pimentos
1 cup yogurt
1 egg
3 tablespoons oil
3 tablespoons scallions

Directions

Preheat the oven to 400°F (200°C). Sift together the dry
ingredients. Cut the pimentos into very small pieces and stir into
dry ingredients. Combine the yogurt, egg, oil, and scallions. Stir
yogurt mixture into dry ingredients until just combined. Pour batter
into a greased 8" skillet. Bake 20 to 25 minutes or until a toothpick
inserted into center comes out clean. Serve warm or cooled. Cut
into wedges. Yield: 6 servings.

30

Afterschool Mini Muffins

Ingredients

3 ounces (75g) cream cheese
1/4 cup peanut butter
2 tablespoons honey
1 egg
1 cup unbleached flour
1/2 cup sugar

1 teaspoon baking soda
1/4 teaspoon salt
2/3 cup milk
1/4 cup vegetable oil
1/2 teaspoon vanilla extract
24 foil miniature baking cups

Directions

Preheat oven to 350°F (180°C). In a small bowl combine the cream cheese, peanut butter, honey, and egg. Beat until smooth and set aside. In a medium bowl, mix together flour, sugar, baking soda and salt. Add milk, oil, and vanilla extract. Beat until smooth, about 1 minute. Spoon the batter into the miniature baking cups, to about 3/4 full. Top each with a teaspoon of cream cheese mixture. Place filled cups on a cookie sheet and bake 20 to 25 minutes. Yield: 24.

31

Apricot Carrot Loaf

Ingredients

1 cup dried apricots
1 1/3 cups unbleached flour
2 tablespoons cornstarch
1 teaspoon baking powder
1/4 teaspoon salt
1/2 teaspoon cinnamon
1/4 teaspoon mace

1/2 cup vegetable oil
2 eggs
3/4 cup sugar
1 teaspoon vanilla extract
1 cup shredded carrot
1/4 cup apricot preserves

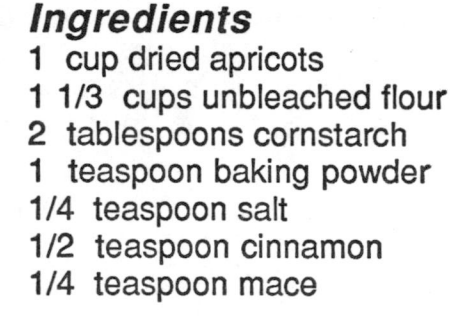

Directions

Preheat oven to 350°F (180°C). Grease and flour a loaf pan. Chop apricots finely. Sift the dry ingredients into a bowl. Set aside. In another larger bowl, beat together the oil, eggs, and sugar until fluffy and lemon colored. Add vanilla. Stir in dry ingredients and mix until smooth. Blend in the carrots and apricots. Pour into the prepared pan. Bake one hour or until a skewer inserted in center comes out clean. Invert onto wire rack to cool. In a small saucepan, warm the apricot preserves with 1 tablespoon water. Use a pastry brush to apply glaze to top of loaf. Yield: 16 servings.

32

Breakfasts

see 38-end

Every Sunday morning around the first of September
for as long as I can remember
my father gets up to make me....AWFUL WAFFLES!
I chew them politely, wash them down with a drink
wishing I could toss them into the sink
because the outsides are mushy, the insides are hard
I know that the batter is goat's milk and lard!

Carob French Toast

Ingredients

2 eggs
1/3 cup carob milk or soymilk
1/2 teaspoon vanilla
1 tablespoon margarine
6 slices of whole-grain bread

Maple Yogurt Sauce

1/2 cup lowfat or nonfat plain yogurt
1 tablespoon of pure maple syrup

Directions

Beat eggs, milk, and vanilla in a large, shallow bowl. Melt margarine in a large skillet over medium heat. Cut bread diagonally and dunk a slice into the batter, covering both sides. Brown the bread on one side, then flip to the other. Remove from pan and top with maple yogurt sauce. Yield: 4 servings.

33

Activity: *Make up a story of your child's possible day and let them fill in the optional endings.*

Applesauce Pancakes

Ingredients

1 cup oatmeal (not instant)
2 cups buttermilk
1 tablespoon sugar
1 teaspoon baking soda
3/4 cup flour
2 eggs
Natural applesauce

Directions

In a large bowl, soak the oatmeal in the buttermilk for about 15 minutes. Sift the sugar, soda, and flour together and stir into the oat mixture. Beat in the eggs, mixing thoroughly, and let stand for 15 minutes. Heat the skillet over medium heat, and brush with oil. Using a 1/2-cup measure, pour out rounds and brown on both sides. Butter the cakes as they are made and keep warm. Put applesauce between two pancakes and cut into wedges.
Yield: 4 servings.

34

Pear Plumps

Ingredients

4 ripe pears
1/3 cup quick-cooking oatmeal
1/3 cup crushed, unsweetened pineapple
2 dried figs, minced
1/4 teaspoon ground cinnamon
1/4 teaspoon pineapple juice concentrate
1 cup apple cider
1 cup natural plain yogurt
1/4 teaspoon almond extract

Directions

Preheat oven to 350°F (180°C). Remove the cores from the pear to 1/2 inch from bottom. Set them upright in a baking dish. Stir together oatmeal, pineapple, figs, cinnamon, and juice concentrate. Stuff the filling into the pear. Pour the apple cider around the pears, cover with foil, and bake for 40 minutes. When pears are done, mix the yogurt, almond extract, and the apple cider that remains on the bottom of the pan and spoon over warm pears.
Yield: 4 servings.

35

Eggs Bennie

Ingredients

6 eggs
6 slices boneless cooked ham
3 English muffins
Hollandaise Sauce
1/2 cup butter, melted
1 egg
1/2 teaspoon dijon mustard
1/2 tablespoon lemon juice

Directions

Fill a medium saucepan with 2 to 3 inches of water. Bring water to a boil. Crack eggs into water and boil until eggs are done to your liking. Toast English muffins, and cut into little pieces. Cut ham Into little pieces. Make hollandaise sauce by putting ingredients into a blender and mixing for 1 minute. Place english muffin and ham pieces on plate, top with egg and hollandaise sauce.
Yield: 6 servings.

36

Hawaiian Toast

Ingredients

4 eggs
8 ounces (225g) crushed
   pineapple, drained
1/4 cup milk
1 tablespoon each maple syrup, sour
   cream, and granulated sugar
8 slices day-old bread
6 tablespoons butter
Powdered sugar
Shredded coconut

Directions

In a blender, whirl eggs, pineapple, milk, syrup, sour cream, and
sugar until smooth. Cut bread slices into shapes and place in a
large shallow dish. Pour egg-pineapple mixture over bread briefly,
then turn to coat other side. In a large frying pan, over medium
heat, melt 2 tablespoons butter. Place a few pieces of bread in pan
and cook until browned on both sides. Dust with powdered sugar
and sprinkle with shredded coconut. Yield: 8 servings.

Buttermilk Oat Cakes

Ingredients

2 cups rolled (not quick-cooking) oats
2 cups buttermilk
1/2 cup unbleached flour
1 tablespoon sugar or honey
1 teaspoon baking soda
3 eggs, lightly beaten
3 tablespoons butter, melted
Plain yogurt mixed with orange juice concentrate

Directions

Combine the oats and buttermilk in a large bowl and put in a cool place to soak overnight. Sift the flour, sugar, and baking soda together in another large bowl. Stir in the oats mixture. Add the eggs and melted butter and beat until thoroughly combined. Heat a skillet until a drop of water dances on the surface. Brush with oil and drop the batter, 2 tablespoons at a time. Bake until browned on the bottom; turn to brown the other side. Top with plain yogurt flavored with orange juice concentrate. Yield 6 servings.

38

Apple Cheese Omelet

Ingredients

2 large tart apples, peeled, cored, and sliced
1 tablespoon lemon juice
1/8 teaspoon each ground nutmeg and cinnamon
3 tablespoons butter

6 eggs
2 tablespoons water
1 cup shredded cheddar cheese

Directions

In a bowl, mix apples, lemon juice, nutmeg, and cinnamon. Melt 2 tablespoons of butter in a frying pan over medium-high heat. Add apple mixture, stirring, just until apples begin to brown. Beat eggs and water. Heat a different frying pan over medium-high heat. Add 1 tablespoon butter and egg mixture. Cook just until omelet is set but still moist on top; lift cooked portion around edge of pan with a spatula to allow uncooked portion to flow underneath. Spoon half the apple mixture and 1/2 cup cheese down center. Fold in half, place on plate, cover with remaining apples and cheese. Cut and serve. Yield: 6 servings.

39

4/7/94 VERY GOOD KARLA ☺

Cottage Cheese Pancakes

Ingredients

3/4 cup large-curd cottage cheese
3 eggs, separated
4 tablespoons flour
4 tablespoons sour cream or plain yogurt
Fresh raspberries or strawberries *or Frozen strawberry jam*
2T sugar
± 1 t oil

Directions

Drain cottage cheese in a sieve until it is dry of all liquid. In a
small bowl, whisk the egg yolks. In a larger bowl, combine the
flour and cottage cheese, mixing thoroughly. Add the yolks and
mix again. Beat the egg whites until stiff, and fold them gently into
the cheese mixture. Heat a skillet to medium and grease lightly.
Drop the batter by scant tablespoonfuls and brown on both sides.
Place a teaspoon of sour cream on each pancake and decorate
with the raspberries. Yield: 4 servings.

40

Yogurt Souffle

Ingredients

2 eggs
2 tablespoons water
2 teaspoons sugar
1 tablespoon butter
2 tablespoons fruit yogurt
Powdered sugar

Directions

Separate eggs and beat egg yolks with water and sugar until pale in color. Whisk egg whites until soft peaks form, then fold through the yolks. Melt butter in a 6-inch omelet pan and pour in the mixture. Level top and cook without moving over medium heat, until the bottom sets. Place under heated broiler to set the top. Spread the yogurt in the center and carefully turn onto a plate, folding the omelet in half. Sprinkle the top with powdered sugar and serve. Yield: 3 to 4 servings.

41

Game: *Play the happy game. Take turns saying what makes you happy.*

Gingerbread Pancakes

Ingredients

1 1/2 cups biscuit mix
1/4 teaspoon ground ginger
1/8 teaspoon ground cinnamon
1/8 teaspoon nutmeg
1 egg, slightly beaten
1 cup milk
1/4 cup light molasses
1 tablespoon margarine

Directions

Stir together baking mix, ginger, cinnamon, and nutmeg. Combine the egg, milk, molasses, and butter in a separate bowl. Add egg mixture to dry Ingredients and beat until smooth. Preheat griddle or frying pan over medium-high heat; grease lightly and pour 1/4 cup batter into pan. Wait until you see bubbles then turn over. Brown both sides and serve with pure maple syrup.
Yield: 12 to 18 pancakes.

42

Tomato Tunnels

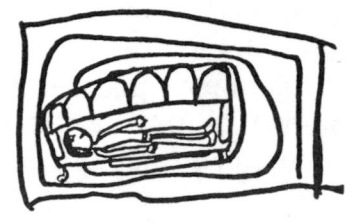

Directions

Preheat oven to 350°F (180°C). Cut tomatoes in half crosswise. Scoop out the pulp from each tomato half, leaving 1/2 inch all the way around. Invert tomato shells on paper towels to drain. Place tomato shells in a pan. Sprinkle with salt and pepper. Break an egg into each tomato and sprinkle 1/2 teaspoon cheese on top. Drizzle 1 teaspoon butter over each. Bake for 20 minutes or until eggs are done the way you like them.
Yield: 4 servings.

Mealtime Question: Ask, "If you could change anything about me, what would you change?"

Ingredients

4 large firm tomatoes
1 teaspoon salt
1/2 teaspoon pepper
8 eggs
4 teaspoons grated parmesan cheese
8 teaspoons butter, melted

Aunt Katie's Coffee Cake

Ingredients

1   cup margarine
2   cups sugar
3   eggs
2   cups unbleached flour
1   teaspoon baking powder
1/2 teaspoon salt
8   ounces (225g) sour cream or
    natural yogurt
1   teaspoon each vanilla, lemon,
    and almond extract
1/2 cup brown sugar
4   teaspoons cinnamon
1   cup ground pecans

Directions

In a large bowl cream margarine and sugar for 8 minutes. Add the eggs, beating in between. Add flour, baking powder, and salt, alternating with the sour cream. Add extracts. Pour 1/2 of the batter into a greased and floured tube or bundt pan. In a separate bowl mix the brown sugar, cinnamon, and pecans. Sprinkle 1/2 of the pecan mixture over the batter. Cover with remaining batter and the rest of the pecan mixture. Bake for 1 hour. Cool the cake in the pan for 5 minutes then transfer to a plate. Yield: 10 to 12 servings.

44

Dutch Roll Ups

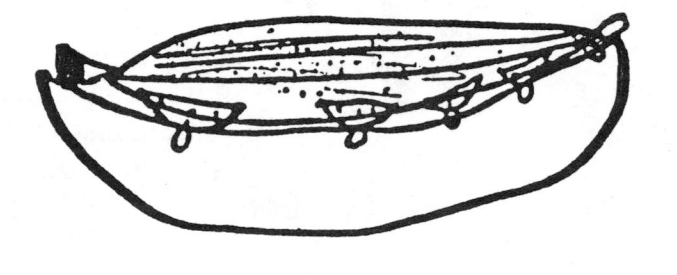

Ingredients
2 cups unbleached flour
1 egg
2 1/2 cups milk
1/2 teaspoon salt
1 tablespoon oil
Berries, coconut, raisins,
banana, sliced apples.

Directions
Put flour into a bowl. Add egg, 2 cups milk, and salt. Beat it
until all the lumps are gone. Gradually add 1/2 cup more milk
to make a thin batter. Cook the pancake in a skillet, making
sure the skillet is hot before pouring the batter in. Put 1
tablespoon oil in skillet and pour batter in to make a very large
circle. Sprinkle fruit on top and press down into the pancake.
Cook a few minutes then flip over and cook other side. Put on
plate. Roll up like a jelly roll and cut into 2 inch sections. Eat!
Yield: 4 servings.

45

German Pancake

Ingredients

1 cup cream-style cottage cheese
6 eggs
1/4 cup milk
1/4 cup vegetable oil
1/2 cup unbleached flour
1/4 teaspoon salt
1 cup chopped, peeled apple

Directions

Place all ingredients except apple in blender. Blend for one minute. Add fruit and stir. Cook on a lightly greased griddle until browned on both sides. Yield: 4 servings.

Note: *Before you eat your meal its nice to remember how lucky you are to have each other!*

46

Blueberries in the Wild

Ingredients

1 cup cooked wild rice
1/2 cup blueberries
1/4 teaspoon nutmeg
2 teaspoons sugar
1/2 cup milk or cream

Directions

Spoon wild rice and blueberries into bowls. Sprinkle with sugar and nutmeg. Pour milk over top and serve. Also tastes yummy warm! Yield: 2 servings.

47

Question: If you could make your Mom try any food, what would you have her try? How about your Dad, brothers, sisters or friends?

Puff Baby

Ingredients
1/2 cup unbleached flour
2 eggs
1/2 cup milk
1/4 cup butter
Powdered sugar
Lemon, cut into wedges

Directions
Preheat oven to 425°F (220°C). Mix flour, eggs, and milk together, leaving batter a bit lumpy. Melt butter in a 9 inch pie plate. Pour batter on top of butter. Bake for 20 minutes or until golden brown and puffy. Sift powdered sugar on top and squeeze lemon to desired amount. Serve at once. Yield: 2 servings.

48

Fruit Surprise

Ingredients

1 banana, peeled
1 cup peeled, chopped peaches
2 cups strawberries, hulled
1/2 cup natural applesauce
1/2 cup pineapple tid-bits
1 tablespoon concentrated
   apple juice

Directions

Place all ingredients in a blender or food processor.
Process briefly, leaving fruit in small chunks. Serve
warm or chilled or serve frozen for afternoon snack!
Yield: 6 servings.

Game: *Play the chore game. Ask your child to tell you how he or she would assign chores in your house. If they do a good job let them assign chores tomorrow.*

49

Ham Cakes

Ingredients

1 3/4 cups unbleached flour
1 teaspoon sugar
3 large eggs
1 3/4 cups milk
2 tablespoons margarine
1/2 pound boiled or canned
        ham, diced
4 tablespoons vegetable oil
Pure maple syrup or natural jelly

Directions

In a large bowl, whisk the flour and sugar into the eggs. Add the milk, beating continuosly. Cover the bowl with a cloth and let stand 2 hours, unrefrigerated. Melt the butter in a heavy skillet over moderate heat. Saute the ham bits until lightly browned. Remove ham from the skillet. Pour 1/2 cup of batter into the skillet and sprinkle with 1/4 of the ham. Bake until brown on the bottom. Turn and brown on the other side. make 3 more pancakes. Put two cakes on top of each other with butter between, like a sandwich. Cut into quarters, cover with syrup or jelly and eat! Yield: 4 servings.

50

Cookies

Busy little fingers
kneading out the dough
baking oatmeal cookies
as fast as they can go.

Flour on the ceiling
thumbprints on the walls
smudges on their faces
batter in the halls.

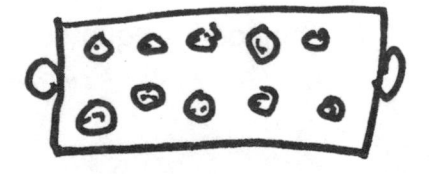

Splashes of vanilla
a dozen eggshells too
cups of powdered sugar
have dropped upon their shoe.

When the fun is over
and they go off to rest
guess whose left behind
to help clean up their mess????

Detective Cookies

Ingredients
1/2 cup white or brown sugar
1/2 cup butter
1 teaspoon vanilla
2 eggs
2 1/2 cups unbleached flour
2 teaspoons baking powder
1/2 teaspoon salt

Directions
Cream sugar, butter, vanilla, and eggs. Mix in flour, baking powder, and salt. Chill dough for 3 hours. Preheat oven to 375°F (190°C). Roll dough out on floured surface. Cut with shaped cookie cutters. Place thumb on top of cookie and press thumb to make a thumb print. Bake 7 to 10 minutes. Yield: 24 cookies.

Note: *Try making a story up about each cookie. Then pretend to be detectives investigating the case! For example, your cookie is working at a toy shop, and is going on a trip. Find out where!*

51

Oatmeal Raspberry Bars

Ingredients

1/2 cup softened butter or margarine
1/2 cup light brown sugar
1 cup unbleached flour
1/4 teaspoon baking powder
1/8 teaspoon salt
1 cup rolled oats
3/4 cups natural raspberry jam

Directions

Preheat oven to 350°F (180°C). Grease a square pan. Mix all the ingredients together except the jam. Press 2 cups of the mixture into the bottom of the pan. Spread the jam close to the edge. Sprinkle the remaining oatmeal mixture over the top and press lightly. Bake 25 minutes and allow to cool before cutting into bars. Yield: 16 - 24 bars.

Note: Try the new fruit-only jam in this recipe for a real taste of summer raspberries. This fruit sweetened jam is not quite as sweet as sugar-sweetened jams - a lot more healthier for kids.

52

Chocolate Pinwheels

Ingredients

1 cup butter or margarine
1 cup sugar
3 eggs
1 teaspoon almond extract
3 cups unbleached flour
1 teaspoon baking powder
1 teaspoon salt
2 tablespoons carob powder
  or unsweetened cocoa

Directions

Preheat oven to 350°F (180°C). Beat butter and sugar in large bowl. Add eggs and almond. Sift in baking powder, salt and flour. Mix with hands until pliable. Divide dough into two balls. Set half on waxed paper. Add 2 tablespoons carob or cocoa to dough, knead together. On lightly floured pastry board roll chocolate and white dough into separate 6-inch long logs. With a rolling pin roll each log into a rectangle. Put chocolate dough on top of white dough and roll up. Cut 1/4" slices and place on greased cookie sheets. Bake 8 to 12 minutes. Yield: 24 cookies.

53

Peanut Kiss Cookies

Ingredients

1 3/4 cups unbleached flour
1 teaspoon baking soda
1/2 teaspoon salt
1/2 cup Crisco shortening
1/2 cup natural peanut butter
1/2 cup white sugar
1/2 cup brown sugar
2 tablespoons milk
1 teaspoon vanilla
Chocolate or carob kisses

Directions

Preheat oven to 350°F (180°C). In bowl mix shortening, peanut butter, and sugars until smooth. Add flour, baking soda, and salt and mix. Add milk and vanilla. Make dough into balls and roll them in sugar. Bake 8 minutes on ungreased cookie sheet. Put chocolate or carob kiss on top and bake for another 3 minutes.
Yield: 24 cookies.

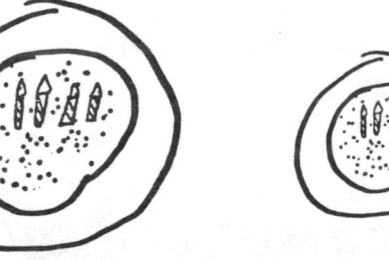

54

Pineapple Bars

Ingredients

15 ounces (425g) unsweetened
    pineapple, undrained
1 1/3 cups peeled, chopped apple
3/4 cup brown sugar
1 1/2 cups unbleached flour
1 teaspoon baking soda
1 egg
1/2 teaspoon salt
1/4 teaspoon ginger

Directions

Preheat oven to 350°F (180°C). Stir together dry ingredients in a large bowl. In another bowl combine remaining ingredients stirring to blend; add egg. Pour over dry ingredients and mix with a fork or wooden spoon until just moistened. Spoon into greased 9x13x2-inch baking pan. Bake 40 minutes. Cool before cutting into squares. Yield: 24 bars.

55

Activity: As you cook make up nonsense sentences like "John sleeps hanging from the ceiling!" Let your child make one up too!

Butterscotch Faces

Ingredients

1/2 cup margarine
1 cup brown sugar
1 egg
1/2 teaspoon vanilla extract
1 1/2 cups whole-wheat
    pastry flour
1 teaspoon baking powder
1/2 cup crushed bran flakes
Raisins, nuts, etc. to decorate

Directions

Preheat oven to 425°F (220°C). Beat margarine until soft and creamy. Blend in brown sugar. Add egg and vanilla. Beat well. Measure flour and baking powder into sugar mixture. Stir until well blended. Stir in cereal. Shape dough into two rolls about 2 inches in diameter. Chill until firm enough to cut. Take dough from refrigerator. Cut into 1/8-inch slices. Let child make faces or designs on circles with decorations. Bake on ungreased baking sheet for 6 minutes. Yield: 24 cookies.

56

Dream Bars

Ingredients

1/2 cup butter
1/2 teaspoon salt
1/2 cup brown sugar
1 cup unbleached flour
1 cup brown sugar
1/2 teaspoon baking powder
1 teaspoon vanilla
2 tablespoons flour
2 eggs, beaten
1 1/2 cups coconut

Directions

Preheat oven to 350°F (180°C). Mix butter, salt, 1/2 cup brown sugar, and 1 cup flour; pat into a 9x13-inch pan. Bake for 15 minutes. Mix 1 cup brown sugar, salt, baking powder, vanilla, 2 tablespoons flour, eggs, and coconut. Blend well. Spread over baked layer. Continue baking for 15 minutes. Cut when warm. Yield: 24 bars.

57

Gingerbread Giants

Ingredients

1 cup molasses
6 tablespoons butter
2 tablespoons water
1/2 cup brown sugar
1 teaspoon each: cinnamon, ginger
1/2 teaspoon each: nutmeg, cloves
1/2 teaspoon baking soda
3 cups whole-wheat flour
1/2 cup powdered milk

Directions

Pour molasses into a small pan. Heat it until it bubbles around the edge. Put butter in mixing bowl and pour molasses on top. Stir. Add water, brown sugar, cinnamon, nutmeg, cloves, ginger, salt, and baking soda. Stir until mixed then add flour and milk. If dough is too sticky add more flour. Dip hands in water and begin to shape your giants. Use raisins, chocolate chips, icing etc. to decorate. Yield: 6 to 8 giants.

58

Note: Play a dancing game while you design your cookies— you can even shape your giants with dancing arms and legs like you!

Oatmeal Pan Cookies

Ingredients

1/2 cup butter or margarine
1 cup brown sugar
2 eggs
2 tablespoons water
1 teaspoon vanilla extract
2 cups uncooked oats
3/4 cup whole-wheat flour
1 teaspoon cinnamon
1/2 teaspoon salt
1/2 cup raisins, coconut,
   sunflower seeds, etc.

Directions

Cream together butter and sugar. Add eggs, water, and vanilla. Stir until well blended. Add oats, flour, cinnamon, and salt. Mix well. Add raisins and any other tasty addition. Place skillet over medium heat. Drop cookie batter by rounded teaspoons onto hot surface and cook both sides until brown, about 4 minutes on each side. Yield: 24 cookies.

59

Puppet Show

Ingredients

1 1/3 cups margarine
2/3 cup sugar
1 teaspoon vanilla
3 1/3 cups unbleached flour
Vegetable food coloring
10 wooden sticks

Directions

Beat margarine until soft. Add sugar and beat until fluffy. Add vanilla. Gradually add flour and beat until mixture resembles coarse crumbs. Divide the dough into several parts, depending on the colors you choose. Add a few drops of color to dough and knead with hands. Form dough into puppet characters, about 1/2 inch thick and 6 inches tall. Carefully insert a stick about 2 inches up. Bake in a 300°F (180°C) for 25 minutes. Cool completely before playing with them. Yield: 12 puppet cookies.

Note: This is a fun party activity— have kids put on a puppet show after their puppets have cooked!

60

Cream Cheese Cookies

Directions

Cream margarine, sugar, egg, cream cheese, buttermilk, and vanilla. Add flour, baking soda, baking powder, and salt. Chill dough for one hour. Preheat oven to 350°F (180°C). Roll dough into balls. Mix the sugar and cinnamon together and put on a plate. Roll dough balls in the cinnamon and sugar. Flatten slightly and bake for 12 to 15 minutes. Yield: 24 cookies.

Ingredients

1/2 cup margarine
1 cup sugar
1 beaten egg
3 ounces (75g) cream cheese
2 tablespoons buttermilk or yogurt
1 teaspoon vanilla
2 cups unbleached flour
1/8 teaspoon baking soda
1/2 teaspoon baking powder
1/2 teaspoon salt
Sugar and cinnamon

61

Chocolate Chippers

Ingredients

1 cup butter or margarine
3/4 cup brown sugar
3/4 cup white sugar
1 egg
1/4 cup sweetened condensed milk
1 teaspoon vanilla
2 1/4 cups unbleached flour
1/2 teaspoon salt
1 teaspoon baking soda
1 cup chocolate or carob chips

Directions

Preheat oven to 350°F (180°C). Cream butter, sugars, egg, condensed milk, and vanilla until fluffy. Mix in flour, salt and baking soda. Add chocolate chips. Drop by tablespoons onto a greased cookie sheet. Bake for 12 to 15 minutes. Yield: 24 cookies.

62

Rice Mallow Bars

Ingredients
1/4 cup butter or margarine
10 ounces (300g) marshmallows
4 cups puffed rice cereal
1/2 cup chocolate or carob chips

Directions
Melt butter in a very large saucepan over medium
heat. Add marshmallows and stir until melted. Add
puffed rice and chocolate chips.   Put into a greased
8x8 inch pan. Wet hands and push down as hard as
you can. Chill before serving. Yield: 24 bars.

Note: *The first candy bar was a Hershey bar produced in 1894.*

63

Miss Ginger Snap

Ingredients
1/2 cup butter
1/4 cup margarine
2 cups brown sugar
2 eggs
1/2 cup molasses
1 teaspoon each, cinnamon, ginger, and nutmeg
3 3/4 cups unbleached flour
2 teaspoons baking soda

Directions
Cream butter and margarine. Beat in sugar. Add eggs and molasses. Stir in remaining ingredients. Chill for several hours. Preheat oven to 350˚F (180˚C). Roll into 1 inch balls. Place on lightly greased cookie sheets. Bake for 8 minutes. Cool and Eat! Yield: 36 cookies.

64

Pie Crust Rolls

Ingredients
2 cups unbleached white flour
1 teaspoon salt
2/3 cup shortening
2 tablespoons butter
4 tablespoons melted butter
1/4 cup sugar
2 teaspoons cinnamon

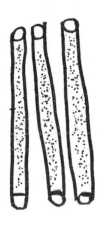

Directions
Preheat oven to 350°F (180°C). Work the shortening and 2 tablespoons butter together with finger tips. Add flour and salt. Cut with a pastry cutter or two butter knives until a dough forms. Roll dough out on a floured surface. Spread melted butter on top of dough and sprinkle sugar and cinnamon mixture over the top. Roll up like a jelly roll, and cut into 1/2 inch wedges. Bake 8 to 10 minutes. This is a good activity for kids to do when you are making a pie! Yield: 24 rolls.

65

Fun Fortune Cookies

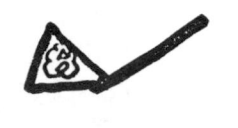

Ingredients

4 tablespoons unbleached flour
2 tablespoons brown sugar
1 tablespoon cornstarch
1 egg white
2 tablespoons vegetable oil
3 tablespoons water
1/2 teaspoon grated orange rind
Pieces of paper with messages, fortunes, or drawings on them

Directions

Mix all ingredients together in a bowl (except paper) and stir until smooth. Grease the skillet or frying pan and place over medium heat. When the skillet is heated drop batter by tablespoons onto skillet forming circles. Cook for 4 minutes, turn batter over, and cook 2 minutes. Quickly remove batter and place the fortune across the center of the cookie, fold in half, then bend over the edge of a bowl. Cool. Yield: 12 cookies.

66

Designer Foods

A pancake is the head
Ten raisins are the toes
Two berries make the eyes
A carrot for the nose

It's not a great Picasso
Sassoon or Calvin Klein
It's just a funny recipe
I call my OWN design

Designer Pancakes

Ingredients
1 1/2 cups lowfat milk
4 tablespoons vegetable oil
2 eggs
2 teaspoons baking powder
1 1/2 cups flour
Oil or margarine for frying

Directions
Put ingredients in bowl and mix. Heat skillet over medium heat, add 2 tablespoons of oil. When a drop of water dances on the surface of the skillet you are ready to begin your art! Using a large spoon dribble the pancake mix into the skillet making a design. Make sure to make your designs small enough to fit inside a pancake. Cook design for 30 seconds. Pour 1/4 cup of the remaining batter on top of the design and cook until browned. Turn pancake and brown. Cover with syrup or jam and eat! Yield: 4 servings.

67

Oatmeal Add-Ons

Ingredients

2 cups water
1 cup rolled oats
1/4 teaspoon salt

Add-ons
Raisins
Coconut
Pineapple tid-bits
Sliced bananas
Any other favorite small food

Directions

Bring salt and water to a boil. Add oatmeal and cook until it begins to thicken (1 to 2 minutes). Reduce heat and simmer for 10 minutes, stirring occasionally. Pour oatmeal into bowls and place on table. Put all the add-on ingredients into small bowls and suggest that your child make a picture on the top of the oatmeal. After picture is complete, stir up the oatmeal and eat. Only one rule to the game; they have to eat their creation! Yield: 4 servings.

68

Tropical Eggs

Ingredients
1/4 cup margarine
15 ounces (425g) pineapple slices
6 eggs
Whole grain toast

Directions
Melt butter in frying pan. Drain pineapple and fry in margarine until lightly browned. Remove from pan and keep warm. Fry eggs, one for each pineapple ring. Remove from pan and arrange on top of pineapple rings. Cut toast into strips and let child spread desired topping. Yield: 6 servings.

Activity: *Suggest making an island treasure map out of the toast strips. Try lying them down to make a path leading to the treasure. The pineapple and egg could contain the treasure!*

69

Collage Melt

Ingredients
Thinly sliced meats
Thinly sliced cheese
Whole grain bread
Tomato
Boiled eggs
Other favorite toppings

Directions
Butter the slices of bread and place face down on a cookie sheet.
Use scissors to cut the meat and cheese into small shapes. Slice
tomato and eggs into small pieces. Have your child decorate each
bread slice making colorful collages. Put the cookie tray under the
broiler for a few minutes until the cheese melts and the shapes all
run together. Cool and eat.

*Activity: After you finish lunch do some stretching exercises
together; up, down, and side to side. Try stretching each other!*

70

Terrific Tomato Soup

Ingredients

1 small can tomato soup
1/4 cup natural lowfat yogurt
Optional Garnishes
popcorn, pretzels, corn chips,
crackers, grated cheese

Directions

In a saucepan, heat the soup according to directions on the can.   When the soup is hot
pour into bowls. Have yogurt and garnishes ready in bowls for your child to create with. If
your child is old enough have them draw a picture or write their name with the yogurt. Use
the other garnishes to complete the design. Yield: 4 servings.

*Activity: This is a good experiment to observe what floats and
what sinks!*

71

Heavenly Star Pizza

Ingredients
Favorite cheese
English muffins, split and toasted
Ketchup or pizza sauce
Optional
Turkey or tofu hot dog slices
Pineapple
Chopped bell pepper
Tomato

Directions
Preheat oven to 350°F (180°C). Cut cheese slices into star shapes with a cookie cutter. For each serving spread muffin half with ketchup or pizza sauce. Let child top pizza with favorite additions.

72

Cracker Crunchies

Ingredients
Favorite assorted crackers
Sliced apple
Sliced cheese
Spread cheese
Berries
Sliced cucumber
Avocado
Hard boiled eggs
Other favorite toppings

Directions
Start with your cracker and let your imagination run free. Children enjoy helping prepare their own party dishes, so let them help create and arrange the cracker tray.

73

Mashed Potato Sculpture

Ingredients
8 potatoes
4 tablespoons butter
4 tablespoons milk
2 teaspoons salt

Directions
Boil potatoes until tender. Cool. Peel and mash with an electric mixer. Add milk, salt, and butter. Let cool in refrigerator. Butter a large baking dish and empty potatoes into it. Using toothpicks, teaspoons, forks, popsicle sticks and clean fingers, form potatoes into shapes. Try animals, faces etc. Beat egg whites slightly and spread over the sculptures with a pastry brush. Bake until brown and shiny. Yield: 6 servings.

Game: Take turns making sounds. Can you guess what the sound is? Oink!

74

Designer Omlettes

Ingredients
1 egg per person
Salt and pepper to taste
Finely chopped tomatoes
Finely chopped cooked ham or chicken
Finely chopped parsley
Grated cheese
Chopped leftover vegetables (optional)

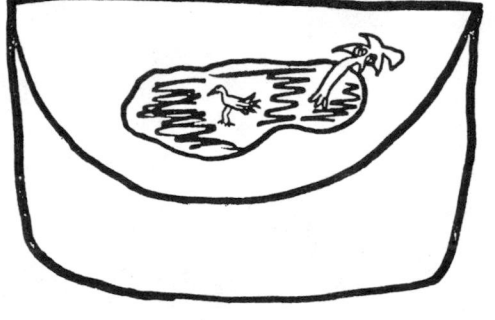

Directions
Preheat skillet. Beat the egg with 1 tablespoon water in a small glass measuring cup. Add salt and pepper to taste. Place the remaining ingredients in separate small bowls. Pour the egg mixture into the skillet and swirl until most of the skillet bottom is covered.

Ask your child to select and then arrange the fillings on top of the egg mixture. Cook for 3 to 5 minutes and then fold the omlette in thirds so that filling is enclosed. Cook for another 2 minutes. There is no need to flip the omlette over. Slide onto a warm plate and serve immediately. Yield: Varies.

75

Food Sculpture

Ingredients
3 ounces (75g) cream cheese
3 tablespoons sour cream
   or plain yogurt
Onion soup mix
Snack foods; chips, pop
corn, pretzels, crackers, etc.

Directions
Warm cream cheese until soft. Blend in 3 tablespoons sour cream
and mix in 1/2 packet of soup mix. Arrange the snacks in piles and
then proceed to build a sculpture, selecting from the assortment of
snacks and cementing them together with the cheese spread. The
cheese doesn't add a lot of strength so it is best to keep the
sculpture low. When finished, your child can have fun eating his or
her creation. Yield: Varies.

76

Clubhouse Sandwiches

Ingredients

8 slices white and wheat bread
An assortment of sandwich fillings
- peanut butter
- lettuce
- tomato slices
- cheese slices
- chicken or turkey
- alfalfa sprouts
- cream cheese
- tuna salad
- egg salad

Directions

Trim the crusts off the bread slices. Place the selected sandwich fillings in individual bowls. Alternate white and wheat bread and let child choose fillings to go between 4 slices. Cut into squares or rectangles and secure each section with a toothpick. Remember to use toothpicks with care! Yield: 16 servings.

77

Tide's Out Sundaes

Ingredients

1 can peaches
1 package jello, any flavor
1 package vanilla pudding mix
1 container non-dairy whipping cream
Toppings, such as coconut, cherries or sprinkles

Directions

Drain can of peaches and reserve liquid. Add cold water to peach juice to make one cup. In a heat-proof pitcher, dissolve jello in 1/2 cup of boiling water. Add juice and water mixture. Pour jello into 4 glasses. Place glasses in fridge tilted so that jello sets diagonally. Just before serving, prepare pudding mix, chop peaches, thaw non-dairy whipping cream, and put toppings in bowls. Remove glasses from fridge and let child layer ingredients according to taste. Yield: 4 servings.

Note: *Fresh fruit in season can be used instead of canned peaches and toppings can include health foods, cereals, finely chopped nuts, and crushed cookies.*

78

Pig's Tails

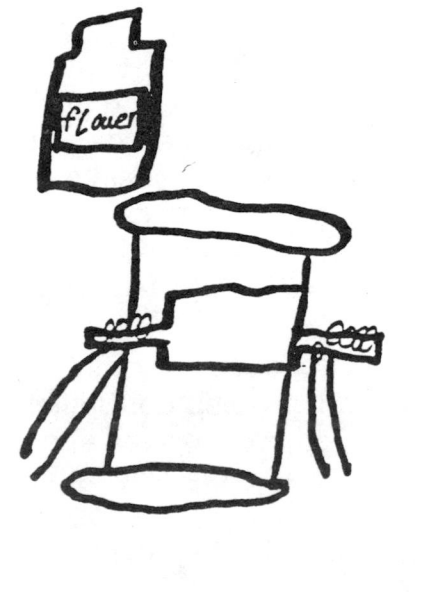

Ingredients
1 package frozen flaky (puff) pastry
1/4 cup sugar

Directions
Preheat oven to 425°F (220°C). Thaw pastry for about 20 minutes. Unfold onto a lightly floured board and roll smooth. Cut into 1/2 inch strips. Have your child roll up the strips into curls or "snails". Place the shapes onto a cookie tray. Sprinkle each shape with the sugar. Bake for 12 minutes or until golden brown. Yield: 6 or more.

79

Layered Vegetable Salad

Ingredients
1 cup broccoli flowerets
1 cup grated carrot
1 cup shredded lettuce
1 cup cauliflower flowerets
1 cup cooked green peas
1 cup creamy herb salad dressing

Directions
Place prepared vegetables in separate bowls. Give each child a clear plastic or glass salad bowl. Alternately layer the vegetables to suit taste with an eye towards design. Spoon salad dressing over top of salad or alternate a layer of dressing with vegetables. Serve with a sandwich and a glass of milk.
Yield: 6 servings.

80

Monkey Bread

Ingredients

1 cup milk, scalded
1 cup cooked potatoes, mashed
1/2 cup vegetable oil
1/2 cup sugar
1 teaspoon salt

1 packet dry yeast
2 eggs, beaten
5 - 6 cups unbleached flour
2 tablespoons butter, melted

Directions

Combine milk, potatoes, oil, sugar, and salt in a large bowl. Dissolve the yeast in 1/2 cup lukewarm water. Add the eggs and the yeast to the potato mixture and stir in 1 1/2 cups of the flour. Mix until well blended. Add the remaining flour until a stiff dough forms. Turn out and knead thoroughly. Return to a greased bowl and turn over. Cover and let rise in a warm place until double in size, about 2 hours. Punch down and divide dough into quarters. Grease a baking dish or tube pan. Pinch off small pieces of dough, roll and dip in melted butter. Arrange in pan in layers. Let rise until double. Preheat oven to 400°F (200°C) and bake bread for 20 to 25 minutes. Serve bread while warm and let the children pull the bread apart to eat. Yield: 10 - 12 servings.

81

Tortilla Towers

Ingredients
1 pound (259g) ground beef
1/2 teaspoon seasoned salt
1 can stewed tomatoes
1 can Spanish tomato sauce
1/2 teaspoon oregano
1 small can green chilies (optional)
16 ounces (500g) cottage cheese
2 eggs
1 can refried beans
8 corn tortillas
2 cups Monterey Jack cheese, grated

Directions
Preheat oven to 350°F (180°C). Brown and drain ground beef. Add salt, tomatoes, sauce, oregano, water, and chilies. Blend and simmer 20 minutes. Cool. Combine cottage cheese and eggs. Empty beans into a bowl. Spread 1 cup of meat sauce in dish. Build towers by alternating meat mixture, cottage cheese mixture, beans, and tortillas. Top with grated cheese. Bake for 30 minutes. Let stand 5 minutes before cutting into wedges. Serve with a salad and Spanish rice. Yield: 8 servings.

82

Kid's Kebabs

Ingredients
Baby onions
Cherry tomatoes
Green pepper
Pineapple chunks
Mushrooms
Grapes
Meat: beef or pork

Marinade
Mix together in a bowl
2 1/2 tablespoons brown sugar
2 tablespoons soy sauce
2 cloves garlic, crushed
1 onion, sliced fine

Directions
Prepare barbeque grill. Make the marinade (see above) and set in
the refrigerator. Cut the meat and green pepper into bite size pieces.
Coat the meat with the marinade. Place all the ingredients in separate bowls and arrange on barbeque table. Give each person a
skewer and let them design their own kebabs. Grill kebabs 4 inches
above coals, about 15 minutes, then slide off onto warm plates-
Serve with couscous and a crisp green salad. Yield: Varies.

83

DESSERTS

Last night in bed about half past eleven
in my dream I traveled to Dessert Heaven.
Creamy cakes and lucious bars
were swinging from the moon and stars.
I entered through a delicious gate
and ate and ate and ate and ate.

Pokies Gelatin Cake

Directions

Preheat oven to 350°F (180°C). Grease and flour 13x9x2 inch baking pan. In a large bowl combine margarine, sugar, and vanilla, beat until well combined. Add eggs. Sift together flour, baking powder, and salt. Alternately add flour mixture and milk to beaten mixture. Pour into pan and bake for 30 minutes. While cake is cooling, prepare gelatin by dissolving in 1 cup boiling water. Add 1 cup cold water to gelatin and stir. Make holes in cake every inch with fork (kids love this job!). Slowly and evenly pour gelatin over cooled cake. Place in refrigerator and chill for 2 hours. Top with whipped topping.
Yield: 16 servings.

Ingredients

1/2 cup margarine
1 3/4 cups sugar
1 1/2 teaspoons vanilla
2 eggs
1 1/4 cup milk
2 3/4 cups unbleached white flour
2 1/2 teaspoons baking powder
1/2 teaspoon salt
3 ounces (85g) package of fruit flavored geletin

84

Sweet Brown Rice Custard

Ingredients

1 cup granola cereal with raisins
1 1/2 cups cooked brown rice
2 cups milk, scalded
2 eggs, lightly beaten
1/3 cup honey or pure maple syrup
2 tablespoons butter or margarine
1 teaspoon vanilla
1/2 teaspoon salt
1/2 teaspoon ground nutmeg

Directions

Preheat oven to 350°F (180°C). Pour cereal into 1 1/2 quart casserole dish. Add the cooked rice to the scalded milk. Stir in the eggs and remaining ingredients. Pour mixture over cereal. Place the casserole into a shallow pan and pour hot water to 1" from the top of the casserole. Bake, uncovered 30 minutes. Stir gently and bake 20 minutes, or until a knife inserted in the center comes out clean. Yield: 6 servings.

85

Apple Crumb Pudding

Ingredients

6 slices natural white bread
1/2 cup butter
3/4 cup brown sugar
5 cups tart green apples
1/4 cup lemon juice
1 teaspoon cinnamon
1/8 teaspoon salt

Directions

Preheat oven to 350°F (180°C). Grease 2-quart casserole dish.
Tear bread into small pieces. Melt butter in a saucepan over low
heat. Remove saucepan from heat and add bread crumbs. Add
brown sugar, cinnamon, and salt to bread crumbs. Peel and slice
apples. Sprinkle apples with lemon juice. Layer apples and
crumb mixture in casserole, ending with crumbs. Pour 1/3 cup
water over apple mixture. Cover and bake covered 1/2 hour, then
uncovered for 1/2 hour. Spoon into dishes and serve with natural
ice-cream or yogurt. Yield: 6 to 8 servings.

86

Strawberry Pie

Ingredients
Crust
1 1/2 cups flour, packed down
1 teaspoon salt
1 tablespoon sugar
3 tablespoons ice water
2/3 cup Crisco shortening
Filling
4 cups strawberries, crushed
1 cup water
3/4 cup sugar
3 tablespoons cornstarch

Directions
Preheat oven to 350°F (180°C). Mix flour, salt, and sugar with spatula. Add the shortening and crumble in, handling as little as possible. Add water as needed to make ball. Roll out dough and put in pie pan. Cook for 10 minutes. Meanwhile, simmer 1 cup crushed strawberries with 2/3 cup water and sugar. Cook until it comes to a slow boil. Remove from heat and gradually add cornstarch that has been mixed with 1/3 cup water. Return to stove and cook until thick. Put berries in crust and pour syrup over. Chill. Yield: 8 servings.

87

Applesauce Yogurt Ice

Ingredients
1 1/4 cups very thick applesauce, chilled
Pinch of grated nutmeg
Pinch of ground cinnamon
1/2 cup powdered sugar
Juice of one orange
1 1/4 cups natural plain yogurt, whipped

Directions
In a bowl, combine the applesauce, nutmeg, cinnamon, and powdered sugar; beat until light. Fold in the orange juice and yogurt. Pour into individual containers, cover and freeze until firm. Transfer to refrigerator about 25 minutes before serving.
Yield 4 servings.

Note: *The Chinese mixed a soft rice paste with milk and froze it, producing the first ice cream.*

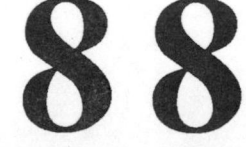

88

Perfect Pavlova

Ingredients

4 egg whites
1/4 teaspoon salt
1 cup sugar
4 teaspoons corn-starch
2 teaspoons vinegar
1 teaspoon vanilla
3 cups diced tropical fruit:
   bananas, kiwis, pineapple etc.
1 cup whipping cream
   or a non-dairy whipped topping

Directions

Preheat oven to 275°F (140°C). Grease and flour a round cake pan. Whip the egg whites with salt until they hold a stiff peak. Add the sugar, one teaspoon at a time, beating until the mixture is stiff and shiny. Beat in the cornstarch, vinegar and vanilla. Put the meringue mixture into the shallow cake pan and hollow out the middle so the edges are about 1/2" above the middle. Bake for 1 1/4 hours or until the meringue is light brown. Cool completely and cover with whipped cream and fruit. Yield: 10 to 12 servings.

89

Peach Crumble

Ingredients

3 cups sliced, peeled peaches
1/2 cup dried currants
1/4 teaspoon nutmeg
1/2 teaspoon cinnamon
1/3 cup oatmeal (not instant)
2 tablespoons butter
2 tablespoons oil
2 tablespoons water

Directions

Preheat oven to 375°F (190°C). Arrange peach slices in a pie pan
(good job for little hands). Sprinkle with currants, cinnamon, and
nutmeg. Combine remaining ingredients in small bowl until
crumbly. Sprinkle crumble over peaches. Bake 35 minutes.
Yield: 8 servings.

Mealtime Question: Who do you think are luckier, boys or girls?

90

Lemon Double Decker Cake

Ingredients

1 cup unsaturated vegetable oil
1 1/3 cup honey
1 cup natural plain yogurt
Rinds of 2 small lemons
1 teaspoon almond extract
4 cups whole wheat pastry flour
(or 1/2 white and 1/2 wheat)
2 teaspoons baking soda

Lemon Icing

1 cup honey
1 teaspoon lemon juice
2 cups milk powder

Directions

Preheat oven to 350°F (180°C).   Measure oil, honey and yogurt into a large bowl and mix well. Grate in the lemon rinds. Add almond extract. Add flour and baking soda. Mix thoroughly. Pour batter into 2 greased 9-inch cake pans and bake for 25 minutes.   While cake is baking, put honey into a blender with lemon juice. Add milk powder a little at a time until icing is thick. Let icing stand for half an hour before icing cake.
Yield: 8 to 12 servings.

91

Fruit Tapioca

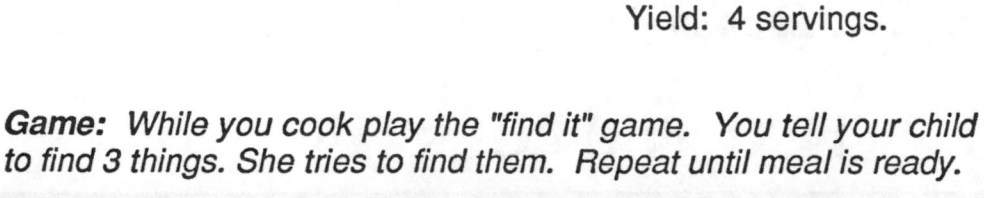

Ingredients

2 1/2 cups apple, raspberry, or
     peach juice
1/4 teaspoon cinnamon
1/4 cup quick-cooking tapioca

Directions

In a saucepan, combine juice and cinnamon.
Stir in tapioca and let it soak for five minutes.
Bring tapioca to a boil over medium heat stirring
frequently. Boil and stir for 2 minutes. Cool 20
minutes and stir. Chill 2 hours before serving.
Yield: 4 servings.

92

Game: *While you cook play the "find it" game. You tell your child*
to find 3 things. She tries to find them. Repeat until meal is ready.

Raspberry Tart

Directions

If using frozen raspberries, thaw, separate carefully, and drain. First prepare pastry. Sift flour into a bowl. Make a hole in the center and add the egg yolk, butter, sugar, and vanilla. Work to a smooth dough. Chill 30 minutes. Preheat oven to 375°F (190°C). Press the dough into a round cake pan. Bake 12 minutes. Take out of oven and sprinkle chocolate chips on top of dough. When they have melted spread like butter. Put jelly in a small saucepan and heat until thin and smooth. Place raspberries on top of chocolate, pour jelly over the top, and chill 2 hours. Top with whipped topping. Yield: 10 to 12 servings.

Ingredients

2 cups raspberries
1/2 cup red currant jelly
1/2 cup non-dairy whipped topping
1/4 cup milk chocolate chips

Pastry

1 cup unbleached flour
1 egg yolk
6 tablespoons butter
6 tablespoons powdered sugar
1/2 teaspoon vanilla

93

Banana Orange Flan

Ingredients

For Pastry
1 1/2 cups unbleached flour
6 tablespoons butter
6 tablespoons sugar
3 egg yolks
1 teaspoon vanilla

For Filling
1/4 cup sugar
2 large oranges
4 ripe bananas
1 cup non-dairy whipped topping

Directions

To make pastry; sift flour into a bowl, make a hole in the center. Add the remaining pastry ingredients and work into a soft dough with fingertips. Chill for 1 hour. Preheat oven to 375°F (190°C). Press dough into a round cake pan and bake 15 minutes. To prepare the filling; put the sugar in a bowl, squeeze the orange juice on top. Slice the bananas into the bowl. After pastry is cool spoon the bananas onto the dough. Mix the remaining juice into the whipped cream. Spread the whipped cream on top of the bananas and eat! Yield: 8 servings.

94

Raisin Surprise Baked Apples

Ingredients

4 cooking apples
4 tablespoons raisins
2 ounces (60g) butter or margarine
4 tablespoons brown sugar
1/2 teaspoon cinnamon

Directions

Preheat oven to 375°(190°C). Wash and core the apples and place in a greased, flat baking dish. Mix together the softened butter, brown sugar, cinnamon, and raisins. Fill the center of each apple with the mixture. Pour about 1/2 cup of water or apple juice around the apples and bake uncovered, for about 30 minutes or until apples are tender. Baste the apples once or twice while cooking. During the last few minutes, place a marshmallow on top of each apple and brown. Yield: 4 servings.

Note: *The best apples for baking whole are Rome Beautys, Granny Smiths, and Pippins. Wash them well before using.*

95

Strawberry Shortcake

Ingredients

4 cups strawberries
1 egg
3/4 cup skim milk
1 teaspoon vanilla
2 tablespoons oil
2 tablespoons butter
1 cup whole wheat pastry flour
3/4 teaspoon baking powder
1/4 teaspoon baking soda
1/4 teaspoon salt
Sugar

Directions

Slice, rinse, and hull strawberries. Put in a bowl and sprinkle a little sugar on top. Preheat oven to 350°F (180°C). Mix together all the other ingredients and spread in a 9x13 inch greased pan. Bake for 35 minutes or until brown. Let cool. Cut into slices and top with strawberries. Yield: 8 to 10 servings.

96

Mealtime Question: *What is good about the way you look? What would you change?*

Bountiful Blueberry Pie

Ingredients

2 cups graham crackers, crushed
4 tablespoons margarine, melted
5 ripe bananas
1 cup lowfat lemon yogurt
1 pint blueberries

Directions

Preheat oven to 375°F (190°C). Mix margarine and graham cracker crumbs. Press into a 9-inch pie pan. Spread blueberries over the crust. Combine the bananas and yogurt in a blender or food processor until smooth. Pour into crust and bake for about 25 minutes. Turn heat off and leave the pie in the oven for an extra 10 minutes. Yield: 8 servings.

97

Fruit Salad Cake

Ingredients

1 each; banana, apple, peach
1 2/3 cups strawberries
2 pineapple slices
3 tablespoons apricot jam
2 tablespoons brandy
3 tablespoons white wine
1/2 ounces (40g) active dried yeast
2 cups unbleached flour
1/2 cup butter, melted
4 eggs separated
2/3 cup sugar
1 teaspoon oil

Directions

Prepare the fruit and cut into small pieces. Place in a large bowl, add the jam, brandy, and wine, stir and leave for one hour. Preheat oven to 400°F (200°C). Sprinkle the yeast over 2 tablespoons warm water and leave until frothy. Sift flour into bowl and stir in melted butter, egg yolks, sugar, and yeast mixture. Beat hard. Beat the egg whites until they are stiff but not dry. Stir the fruit salad into the dough, then fold in the egg whites. Pour into a greased and floured shallow flan pan. Bake for 40 minutes.
Yield: 8 servings.

98

Strawberry Pudding

Ingredients

1/2 cup strawberries, washed and hulled
2 tablespoons honey
1/4 cup maple syrup
5 ounces plain lowfat yogurt
2 egg whites

Directions

Place strawberries In a blender or food processor, with honey, syrup, and yogurt. Puree until smooth. Chill for one hour or until ready to serve. Beat egg whites on high speed until stiff peaks are formed. Fold the egg whites into the strawberry mixture. Spoon into dessert dishes. Serve immediately. Yield: 4 servings.

99

Mealtime Question: Ask your child to name every piece of clothes they had on today. What colors were they?

Do It Yourself

Marshmallow Meatloaf
Gravy with Cherries
Chocolate Potatoes
Broccoli and Berries

Alone in the kitchen
Busy as elves
Cooking a dish
they created themselves.

Maley Milkshake

Ingredients

1 cup lowfat milk
3 scoops natural vanilla ice-cream
2 teaspoons natural jam, carob powder, or chocolate sauce

Yield: 3 to 4 servings.

Directions

1. Wash hands before starting.
2. Get out all ingredients.
3. Put all ingredients into a blender and blend on medium high speed for 2 to 3 minutes.
4. Pour into glasses and enjoy.

Note: In Literacy Begins at Birth Dr Marjorie Fields explains that taking time to read to your children almost assures that they will later love to read. (Tucson: Fisher Books: 1989), p. 6. Research shows that good readers were read to when they were little.

100

Cinnamon Toast

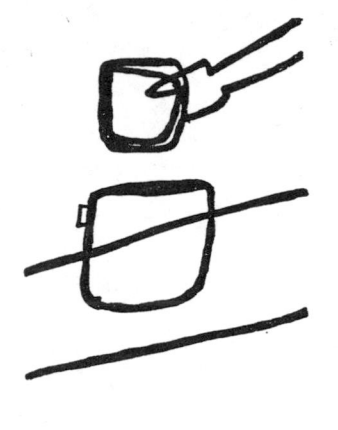

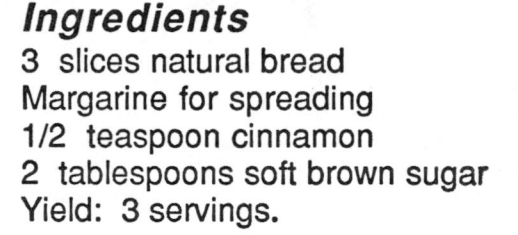

Ingredients
3 slices natural bread
Margarine for spreading
1/2 teaspoon cinnamon
2 tablespoons soft brown sugar
Yield: 3 servings.

Directions
1. Wash hands before starting.
2. Get out all ingredients.
3. Put toast in toaster
4. While the toast cooks mix the cinnamon and sugar together.
5. When toast is done, spread with margarine
6. Sprinkle sugar mixture on top.
7. Eat!

101

Boiled Eggs

Ingredients
Fresh eggs
Whole grain bread
Margarine or natural jam

Directions
1. Wash hands before beginning.
2. Get out all ingredients.
3. Put eggs in a medium size saucepan. Cover them with cold water.
4. Bring water to boil over high heat.Reduce heat and simmer (barely boiling) for desired time.
   Soft eggs- 3 minutes
   Medium eggs- 5 minutes
   Hard boiled eggs- 20 minutes
5. Remove from heat. Cover eggs with cold water.
6. Put toast in toaster, either peel egg or crack in half with spoon. Eat with toast.

102

Homemade Cheese

Ingredients

1 quart (1 litre) milk
1 lemon
Strainer
Cheesecloth

Directions

1. Wash hands before starting.
2. Get out all ingredients.
3. Pour milk into a saucepan and cook over medium heat until it just boils. Be careful not to let it boil over.
4. Add the juice of the lemon and let the milk separate into curds and whey.
5. Pour through a strainer so that the curds are left behind.
6. Squeeze all the moisture out of the curds by emptying into a piece of cheese cloth, forming a ball, and twisting. Chill.
7. Spread on crackers or bread.

103

Dumpling Soup

Ingredients

Chicken or beef broth
1 pound (450g) ground meat
3 egg
1 teaspoon salt
1/4 cup bread crumbs
2 tablespoons soft butter
6 tablespoons whole-wheat flour
1/2 cup grated cheese

Directions

1. Wash hands before starting.
2. Get out all ingredients.
3. Heat broth in a large pot until boiling.
4. Combine ground meat, 1 egg, 1/2 teaspoon salt, and bread crumbs. Shape the meat mixture into little balls.
5. Make the cheese dumplings by combining butter, 2 eggs, flour, grated cheese, and 1/2 teaspoon salt. Make cheese dumplings into little balls.
6 When the broth is boiling drop meat and cheese dumplings into soup by teaspoons. When they float to the top they are done (about 10 minutes). Eat and enjoy!

104

Blueberry Pancakes

Ingredients
1 cup unbleached flour
1 egg
1 1/4 cups milk
Pinch of salt
1 cup fresh blueberries
Butter for frying

Directions
1. Wash hands before starting.
2. Get out all ingredients.
3. Put flour and salt in a bowl.
4. Add egg and half of milk, mix well.
5. Add the rest of the milk.
6. Put 2 tablespoons butter in frying pan over medium heat.
7. Drop pancake batter by large spoonfuls into pan.   Drop berries onto pancake. When pancake bubbles it is time to turn it over. Put on plate, dust with powdered sugar or maple syrup.

105

Egg Nests

Ingredients

1 1/4 pounds (575g) ground meat
1/2 cup bread crumbs
4 tablespoons grated parmesan cheese
4 mashed potatoes
8 eggs
7 tablespoons melted butter
Salt and pepper to taste
Yield: 8 servings

Directions

1. Wash hands before starting
2. Get out all ingredients.
3. Preheat oven to 350°F (180°C).
4. Mix meat, bread crumbs, cheese, mashed potatoes, salt, and pepper in a bowl.
5. Make nests by forming 8 balls out of meat. Flatten and make a depression in center.
6. Place in buttered oven proof dish and cook for 35 minutes.
7. Remove from oven, crack egg in nest, sprinkle with salt, return to oven for 10 minutes.

106

Yogurt Fruit Shake

Ingredients
1/2 cup natural fruit yogurt
1 cup natural fruit juice
8 ice cubes
Banana (optional)
Yield: 3 servings

Directions
1. Wash hands
2. Put ingredients into a blender and blend on medium for 3 minutes or until ice is smooth.
3. Pour into glasses and enjoy!

Note: *Parents should understand that scribbling is an important first stage of writing. Your child must go through this stage to get to the next one. Provide crayons, paper and a suitable environment and actively encourage your child to scribble. You can try it too!*

107

Yummy Parfaits

Ingredients

4 cups fresh fruit
1 cup whipped topping
2 small boxes instant pudding
Garnishes; raisins, coconut,
nuts carob chips, etc.
Yield: 6 to 8 servings.

Directions

1. Wash hands before starting.
2. Get out all ingredients.
3. Get out dessert or wine glasses.
4. Make pudding.
5. Prepare fruit, wash and cut into small pieces.
6. Put garnishes in readily available piles.
7. Begin layering pudding, fruit, garnishes in any way you like. Be creative! Top with whipped topping. Serve to Mom or Dad.

108

Grilled Peanut Butter Sandwich

Ingredients

8 slices whole grain bread
Natural peanut butter
Margarine
Natural fruit jam

Directions

1. Wash hands.
2. Get out ingredients.
3. Spread margarine on eight slices of bread. Place margarine side down on clean surface.
4. Spread peanut butter on four slices of bread. Spread jam on four slices of bread.
5. Put peanut butter and jam slices together.
6. Put frying pan over medium heat. Place sandwiches in frying pan.
7. Fry on one side until golden brown. Turn with spatula and fry on other side.

109

Berries and Cream

Ingredients

1 pint strawberries, raspberries,
   or blueberries
1 cup plain natural yogurt
6 tablespoons brown sugar
Yield: 4 servings.

Directions

1. Wash hands before starting.
2. Get all ingredients out.
3. Clean fruit, pull off green tops and cut into
   small pieces (if using strawberries).
4. Put fruit into a pretty bowl.
5. Put yogurt on top of the fruit and mix.
6. Sprinkle brown sugar on top.

grapes
sour cream
brown sugar

110

Fruit Flake Chicken

Ingredients

4 large boneless, skinless, chicken breasts
2 tablespoons margarine
2 tablespoons natural peanut butter
3/4 cup peach or apricot juice
2 cups cornflakes, crushed
Yield: 4 servings.

Directions

1. Wash hands before starting.
2. Get out all ingredients.
3. In a shallow pan, mix peanut butter, margarine, and juice.
4. Place the chicken pieces in the juice pan and refrigerate for one hour.
5. Preheat oven to 350°F (180°C).
6. Pour the cornflakes onto a sheet of waxed paper and roll the chicken one piece at a time, covering well.
7. Place chicken on a cookie sheet that has been covered with foil. Top each chicken piece with 1 tablespoon of the leftover juice.
8. Bake 45 minutes.

111

Pancake Soup

Directions

1. Wash hands before starting.
2. Get out all ingredients.
3. Break the egg in a bowl.
4. Add the flour, parsley, parmesan cheese, half and half, and milk. Beat with a fork.
5. Butter a frying pan, place on medium heat. When ready pour 1/2 cup batter into pan like a thin pancake.
6. After 2 minutes turn over and cook other side.
7. Bring soup stock and peas to boil in large pot.
8. Roll pancakes up, and cut across making long thin strips.   Put them in soup and eat!

Ingredients

1 egg
3/4 cup unbleached flour
1 teaspoon parsley
1 tablespoon grated Parmesan cheese
1 tablespoon half and half
1 1/4 cups milk
3/4 cup peas
5 tablespoons butter
4 cups soup stock
Yield: 4 servings.

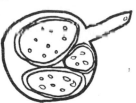

112

Funny Fettuccine

Ingredients

1/2 stick butter at room temperature
1/4 cup cream
1/2 cup grated parmesan cheese
6 quarts water
1 tablespoon salt
12 ounces(340g) fettuccine or egg
    noodles
Yield: 6 to 8 servings.

Directions

1. Wash hands before beginning.
2. Get out all ingredients.
3. Cream the butter.
4. Stir in the cream and cheese.
5. In your biggest pan, boil the water. Add the salt.   Be sure to point pan handles toward the wall.
6. Add the noodles and stir gently. Cook uncovered for 8 minutes. Drain.
7. Add the butter-cheese mixture. Stir until the noodles are covered.
8. Put on large plate. For fun cut up some veggies and make funny faces on top of the pasta.

113

Fish In A Blanket

Ingredients

1 pound (900g) sole
6 slices boiled ham
1 lemon
6 teaspoons parmesan cheese
Tinfoil
Yield: 6 servings.

Directions

1. Wash hands before starting.
2. Get out all ingredients.
3. Read through recipe.
4. Preheat oven to 400°F (200°C).
5. Cut fish into 6 pieces.
6. Place one fish filet on top of ham slice.
7. Squeeze lemon juice on each fish.
8. Sprinkle 1 teaspoon parmesan cheese over fish.
9. Roll up ham with fish in it.
7. Wrap each fish roll in tinfoil and seal it tight.
8. Put rolls in a pan and bake for 35 minutes.

114

Lilly's Layered Bars

Ingredients

1/2 cup margarine
1 cup graham cracker crumbs
1 cup flaked coconut
3/4 cups chocolate or carob chips
3/4 cups butterscotch chips
1 can sweetened condensed milk
Yield: 24 bars.

Directions

1. Wash your hands.
2. Get out all ingredients.
3. Preheat oven to 325°F. (170°C).
4. Melt margarine in saucepan over low heat.
5. Pour margarine into 13 x 9 inch baking pan, covering bottom evenly.
6. Add in layers: graham cracker crumbs, coconut, chocolate chips, butterscotch chips, and condensed milk.
7. Bake 30 minutes.
8. Cut into squares while still warm!

115

FOREIGN FOODS

Turn on the music
dim the lights low
light pretty candles
knead out the dough
cook spicy pasta
on a plate piled high

then serve alongside
a fat pizza pie.
Feel like a restaurant
in the city of Rome
without having to travel
far from your home.

French Crepes Suzette

Ingredients

2 tablespoons unbleached flour
3 eggs
1 tablespoon sugar
1/4 teaspoon salt
1 tablespoon milk
1 tablespoon butter, melted

Directions

Place the flour, eggs, sugar, salt and milk into a bowl and whisk until mixture is smooth. Add melted butter. Mix until smooth. Pour 3 tablespons of batter into hot frying pan or small cast iron pan. Tilt to cover bottom of pan. Cook 1 minute then flip over. Cook 1/2 minute on other side. Remove from pan and stack on a warm platter. Yield 4 servings.

Note: *Here is a delicious sauce to try. Beat until fluffy - 1 stick softened butter, grated rind of 2 oranges, juice of 1 orange, and 6 tablespoons sugar. Place each crepe in sauce, coat both sides and fold into quarters.*

116

Nasi Goreng

Ingredients

1 package frozen peas and carrots
1 pound pork or chicken
2 tablespoons vegetable oil
1 onion, peeled and chopped
4 cups cooked rice

2 tablespoons soy sauce
1/4 teaspoon sage
5 drops tabasco
Pepper and salt to taste
1 egg, beaten

Directions

Cook the peas and carrots, drain and set aside. Cut meat into very small pieces. Melt 2 tablespoons oil or butter in a frying pan. Add meat and onions and brown. Add rice, soy sauce, sage, tabasco, salt and pepper. Cook slowly and stir frequently for 15 minutes. Add peas and carrots and cook for another 5 minutes. Make a hole in center and pour in egg. Stir until set. Cut egg mixture into strips and lightly mix into the rice mixture. Serve with slices of tomato and cucumber. Yield: 6 servings.

Note: Nasi Goreng comes from the Dutch East Indies which is now called Indonesia.

117

German Raisin Crepes

Ingredients

1/3 cup golden raisins (sultanas)
5 tablespoons hot water
3 eggs
1 cup milk
1 3/4 cups flour
3 tablespoons sliced almonds
Powdered sugar

Directions

In a small bowl combine raisins and water and let stand 5 minutes. In medium bowl, beat together eggs and milk and then beat in flour. **Let stand 15 minutes.** Stir in raisins and almonds. Heat a small amount of butter in a frypan. Spoon batter for 1 crepe into pan. Cook until golden brown, and flip over. Using 2 forks, tear crepe into pieces. Cook a little longer. Sprinkle with powdered sugar. Keep warm. Repeat with remaining batter. Serve in individual bowls with fresh or stewed apples. Yield: 6 servings.

*Note: A pudding, such as these crepes or **kaiserschmarren**, is served at the end of a traditional German-family meal, particularly if children are present.*

118

Scotch Eggs

Ingredients
1 pound (500g) ground beef or pork
1 cup bread or cracker crumbs
1 tablespoon tomato or steak sauce
5 eggs
1/2 onion, finely chopped

Directions
Preheat oven to 350°F (180°C). Hard boil 4 eggs. Mix the meat, 1/2 cup breadcrumbs, sauce, onion, and 1 raw egg. Season with salt and pepper. Divide the mixture into quarters. Flatten each portion to make a circle about the size of a saucer. Place a shelled egg in the center of each circle. Fold over the meat to completely cover the egg. Roll in remaining breadcrumbs. Bake in a greased roasting dish for 30 minutes, turning. To serve, cut in half and garnish with a sprig of parsley.
Yield: 8 servings.

Note: Bake potatoes in same dish and serve with broiled tomatoes - halved and topped generously with parmesan cheese.

119

Kiwi Krisps

Ingredients
1/2 cup butter or margarine
1/3 cup sugar
1 tablespoon sweetened condensed milk
1 1/4 cups unbleached flour
1 teaspoon baking powder
4 ounces (125g) dark chocolate

Directions
Preheat oven to 375° F (190°C). Soften butter and blend in the sugar. Add condensed milk and beat. Stir in sifted dry ingredients. Chop or grate chocolate into small chunks and add to flour mixture. Stir to blend. Take teaspoonfuls of dough and roll into balls. Place on cookie tray. Press balls with a fork. Bake for 20 minutes or until light brown.
Yield: 36 cookies.

Note: *New Zealanders call themselves Kiwis after their native bird. These cookies are favorites of New Zealand children. Long before chocolate chips were available in stores, cooks used blocks of chocolate for all chocolate dishes, cakes, and cookies.*

120

Pirate's Paella

Ingredients

4 chicken breasts, boned and cut up
1 onion
1 green pepper, chopped
2 tomatoes, peeled and chopped
1/2 teaspoon saffron or tumeric
2 cloves garlic, crushed

Salt and pepper
2 cups long grain rice
4 cups chicken broth
1 pound (500g) cooked shrimp
8 cooked clams
1 cup frozen peas

Directions

In an electric frying pan brown the chicken breasts in 3 tablespoons vegetable oil until golden. Remove from pan. Add chopped onion and saute until brown. Add green pepper, tomatoes, saffron, garlic and salt and pepper to taste. Simmer for 5 minutes, stirring occasionally. Stir in rice. Add chicken, clams, and shrimp. Pour chicken broth over rice mixture and stir lightly. Cover and cook gently for 30 minutes. Sprinkle peas over top, cover and cook another 10 minutes or until liquid is absorbed and rice is tender. Yield: 8 servings.

121

Oriental Pork Stir-fry

Ingredients
1 pound (500g) lean pork
1 bunch bok choy
1 small can water chestnuts
1 cup fresh mushrooms
3 green onions
1 tablespoon vegetable oil

Sauce:
1 cup chicken broth
1/4 cup soy sauce
2 tablespoons dry sherry
2 tablespoons cornstarch
1/4 teaspoon garlic powder
1/4 teaspoon ground ginger

Directions
Cut pork into 1/4 inch strips. Slice bok choy, water chestnuts, mushrooms, and onions. Heat oil in wok or frying pan. Add pork to hot oil and stir-fry 3 to 5 minutes until light brown. Remove to a plate. Add vegetables to wok and stir-fry 4 to 5 minutes. Combine sauce ingredients. Pour over vegetables. Add pork. Heat through for about 3 minutes more, stirring constantly, until thickened. Serve over rice or noodles.
Yield: 4 - 6 servings.

Note: *Use this meal to learn how to use chopsticks. The Chinese word for chopsticks is kwai-tsze and means "quick ones" because food can be eaten more quickly if you don't have to cut it up first.*

122

Chapattis

Ingredients
1 cup whole-wheat flour
1 cup unbleached flour
1/4 teaspoon salt
1 tablespoon butter, clarified

Directions
Sift the flours and salt together. Stir in 1/2 cup water and the butter. Knead to make a stiff dough. Let the dough stand, uncovered, for an hour. Knead again and form into small balls the size of walnuts. Roll each dough ball into very thin circles on a floured board. Bake on a preheated griddle or frypan over low heat. Turn chapattis often until both sides are light brown, but not hard. Serve with curry or stew. Yield: 12.

Note: *The Indians of India use chapattis instead of utensils. Let your child try this way of eating - scooping the food up with a chapatti.*

123

Dim Sims

Ingredients
1 pound (500g) ground pork
2 teaspoons soy sauce
1/4 teaspoon pepper
1/2 cup mushrooms, cooked
1 1/2 teaspoons sugar
1 package of won ton wrappers

Directions
Combine all ingredients except wrappers.
Separate wrappers and place 1 tablespoon
of the mixture in center of each. Follow the
directions on the wrapper package to wrap up
meat mixture. Steam for 30 minutes. Yield: 40.

*Note: For less fat, substitute ground lean turkey for ground pork.
Serve the dim sims with white rice and stir-fried vegetables.*

124

Moroccan Couscous

Ingredients
1 cup coucous
1 1/2 cups water
1/2 teaspoon salt
1 tablespoon butter or margarine

Directions
In a saucepan, bring water, salt, and butter to a boil. Stir in couscous and cover. Remove from heat and let stand for 5 minutes. Fluff couscous lightly with a fork before serving. Mound couscous on serving platter and make a hole in the center. Fill with stewed meats, chicken, or vegetables. Also great with kebabs. Yield: 4 servings.

Note: Couscous is the favorite dish of families in North Africa. It is really a fine-grained semolina cooked so that each grain is separated.

125

Cornish Pasties

Ingredients

3 cups unbleached flour
1/4 teaspoon salt
1/2 cup butter or margarine
4 tablespoons cold water
1/2 pound (250g) lean beef

1 small potato, peeled
1 carrot, chopped
1 small onion, chopped
1/2 cup peas
1 egg white, slightly beaten

Directions

Preheat oven to 450°F (230°C). Make pastry by sifting together flour and salt and rubbing in the butter until mixture is crumbly. Add enough cold water to form dough into a ball. Chill. Dice meat and potato. Combine with other vegetables. Roll out pastry very thin and cut out 8 circles, 6 inches in diameter. Spoon 1/8 of filling onto center of each circle. Dampen edges then fold pastry in halves. Crimp edges to seal. Brush with egg white. Slash pastry to allow steam to escape. Bake for 10 minutes. Reduce heat to 350°F (180°C) and bake for 30 more minutes or until pastry is golden brown. Cool 10 minutes before serving. Yield: 8 servings.

126

Beef Sate and Silky Sauce

Ingredients

1   pound (500g) sirloin steak
2   tablespoons soy sauce
1 1/2   tablespoons honey
2   cloves garlic, crushed
1 1/2   teaspoons coriander
1 1/2   teaspoons caraway seed
1/4   teaspoon chili powder
1   cup coconut milk

Silky Sauce

Combine 1/2 cup light brown sugar, 1/2 cup soy sauce, 2 tablespoons lime juice, 1/3 cup grated onion and 1/2 teaspoon freshly ground pepper. Heat until sugar is dissolved.

Directions

Combine all ingredients except meat in a deep bowl. Slice steak in 1 inch cubes and add to liquid. Marinate for at least an hour, then thread onto skewers. Grill over hot coals, turning 2 or 3 times, for about 10 minutes. Baste with marinade before and during cooking. Remove from the skewers onto a warm plate and serve with the sauce above.

Note: In Malaysia, sate (pronounced sahtay) is dipped in the sauce and served with steamed bok choy or pea pods and large bowls of fluffy rice.

127

Katrina's Kasha

Ingredients
2 cups broth, consomme or bouillon
1/2 teaspoon salt
1/4 teaspoon pepper
2 tablespoons butter or margarine
1 egg, slightly beaten
1 cup buckwheat or Kasha

Directions
Combine the broth, salt, pepper, and butter in a saucepan and bring to a boil. In a bowl, mix together the beaten egg and buckwheat until all the kernels are moistened. Place the kernels in a frying pan and cook on high heat, stirring constantly, until kernels are dry and separate, about 3 minutes. Quickly add the boiling liquid and cover frying pan. Reduce heat to low and steam kernels for 10 minutes. Remove cover, fluff with a fork, and serve warm. Yield: 6 servings.

Note: Kasha, also known as buckwheat or groats is a fine source of protein. It is a favorite food of Russian children.

128

Italian Chicken Risotto

Ingredients
1/4 cup minced onion
2 tablespons olive or vegetable oil
3 tablespoons butter or margarine
1 1/2 cups uncooked rice
4 cups chicken stock
1 1/2 cups cooked and shredded chicken
1/2 cup parmesan cheese

Directions
Lightly brown the onion in heated oil and butter. Add rice and stir until the rice turns white. Add the stock slowly stirring frequently. Keep the mixture bubbling as the stock is added. Stir in the chicken with the last of the stock. When the rice is done, in 20 to 30 minutes, stir in the cheese. Season with salt and pepper and serve immediately. Sprinkle with additional parmesan cheese if desired. Yield: 6 - 8 servings

Note: *This recipe is also good with leftover cooked turkey.*

129

Quesadillas

Ingredients
3 6-inch (150mm) flour tortillas
Vegetable cooking oil
1 cup shredded white cheese
1 cup shredded yellow cheese
1/2 cup finely chopped tomato
Parsley or cilantro leaves

Directions
Lightly fry each tortilla in 1/4 inch of hot oil until crisp and golden, turing once. Drain on pa-per towels. Sprinkle with combined cheeses and top with tomato. Microwave on HIGH 1 minute or until cheese is melted. Cut each tortilla into quarters. Garnish with parsley or cilan-tro leaves. Serve warm. Yield: 3 servings.

Note: *If using a conventional oven, place tortillas on a cookie sheet and bake at 350°F (180°C) for 10 minutes or until cheese is melted.*

130

Latkes

Ingredients

5 medium potatoes
1 tablespoon lemon juice
2 eggs
1/4 cup flour
1 small onion, chopped
1/3 cup parsley, chopped
1/2 teaspoon salt
1/4 cup vegetable oil

Directions

Peel and coarsly grate potatoes. Half fill a large bowl with water to which lemon juice has been added. Soak potatoes in bowl. Beat together eggs, flour, onion, parsley and salt in another bowl. Remove handfuls of potatoes, squeezing out all the water. Add to egg mixture. When all potatoes are added, mix well. In a frying pan, heat oil. Spoon batter into pan and flatten each pancake with spatula into a 3 inch round. Turn once when brown. Drain on paper towels and keep warm until ready to eat. Yield: 12 - 15.

131

Fr🍓its

Little green banana
so good for my health
sitting very proudly
upon my kitchen shelf

Sunning by the window
feeling sweet and mellow
passing each day
without turning yellow

Little green banana
It was so nice to meet you
But now that we've met
I don't think I can eat you!

Fruity Banana Split

Ingredients
4 bananas
2 cups cottage cheese
Large can of fruit cocktail

Directions
Cut each banana into 4 pieces. Put them into a bowl. Put 1/2 cup of cottage cheese on top of the bananas. Cover generously with the fruit cocktail. This is a nice play snack for kids to help make. Yield: 4 servings.

Note: Words are less important than the judgements that accompany them, according to Dorothy Carkille Briggs, teacher of parent-education. She writes in her book, Your Child's Self Esteem, (New York: Doubleday, 1975) that the child's own judgement of herself emerges from the judgements of others and the more she likes her self-image, the higher her self-esteem. (p. 19)

132

Apple Fritters

Ingredients

4 cooking apples
1 1/4 cups sifted unbleached flour
1/2 teaspoon baking powder
2 tablespoons sugar
2 eggs, separated
1/2 cup milk

Directions

Cut apples into small chunks. Sift together the flour, baking powder, and sugar. Beat egg yolks and milk together and add to dry ingredients. Add apples. Beat egg whites until stiff

Beat egg whites until stiff and fold into flour mixture. Drop tablespoons of batter into hot oil and cook until golden on both sides. Serve hot sprinkled with cinnamon sugar. Make cinnamon sugar by mixing 1 teaspoon cinnamon with 1/4 cup sugar. Yield: 12 servings.

133

Cranberry Sherbert Delight

Ingredients

1 cup crushed pineapple, drained
1 can whole cranberry sauce
1 cup sour cream or plain yogurt
1/4 cup honey

Directions

Mix together the pineapple and cranberry sauce. Blend the sour cream and honey and add to fruit mixture. Stir. Pour mixture into a freezer tray and freeze until slushy. Remove from freezer and beat. Refreeze until firm. To serve, turn out and cut into shapes. Yield: 4 servings.

Note: *Throughout time children have loved stories, rhymes, and singing games. Recall the ones from your own childhood and share them with your children. They in turn, will share them with their children.*

134

Gooseberry Flan

Ingredients

1   deep dish frozen pie crust
2   cups gooseberries, prepared
2   eggs, beaten
2   teaspoons flour
1   tablespoon butter, melted
1/2 cup sugar

Directions

Prepare gooseberries by removing the tiny stalks and tops.
Preheat oven to 400°F (200°C). Cover pie crust with fresh
gooseberries. Mix together (in a blender) the eggs, flour, butter,
and sugar. Pour over fruit. Bake for 10 minutes and then for 30
minutes at 350°F (180°C). Serve with non-dairy whipped cream
or vanilla ice cream. Yield: 6 servings.

135

Fall Fruit Medley

Ingredients

1 can pineapple chunks
3 apples, cored and chopped
3 oranges, peeled and cut up
1 cup green grapes
1 cup red grapes
2 bananas, peeled and sliced
1 cup chopped nuts and raisins
1/2 each honey and plain yogurt

Directions

Drain pineapple and reserve juice for dressing. Place all the fruit in a large bowl and toss to mix. Arrange on bed of Fall leaves which have been rinsed and patted dry. Make dressing by blending pineapple juice, honey, and yogurt. Pour over fruit before serving. Yield: 6 servings.

Note: Yogurt is natural and provides needed friendly bacteria for digestion. It is known by other names too. Kifir is from camel's milk and kumiss is from mare's milk. Most yogurt today is made from cow's milk, although originally it was from ewe's milk.

136

Hot Apple Scrunch

Ingredients

4 cups cooking apples, cored and sliced
1/2 cup currants
1/4 cup honey
1 teaspoon cinnamon
Juice of 1 lemon
1/2 cup apple juice

Topping

1/2 cup melted butter
2 teaspoons cinnamon
1 teaspoon vanilla
2 cups oatmeal

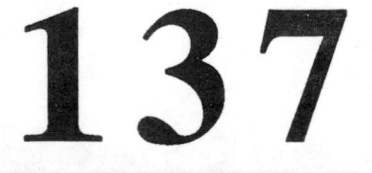

Directions

Preheat oven to 350°F (180°C). Mix all ingredients and put in a greased baking dish. Add extra apple juice to barely cover apples. Combining topping ingredients and sprinkle over apples. Bake for 40 minutes or until crust is golden brown. Yield: 6 servings.

137

ANZAC Fruit Bars

Ingredients

1 cup cooking oats
1 cup unbleached flour
1/2 cup brown sugar
1/2 cup coconut
1/2 cup dried apricots, chopped
1/2 cup raisins
1 teaspoon baking soda
2 tablespoons warm water
1/2 cup butter or margarine
1 tablespoon molasses

Directions

Preheat oven to 350°F (180°C). Place the oats, flour, sugar, coconut, apricots, and raisins in a bowl and stir. Dissolve the baking soda in the water. Melt the butter and molasses together and add to dry ingredients with the water and soda. Mix until blended. Press mixture into a greased square or rectangular pan. Bake for 20 minutes or until golden brown. Remove from oven and cool 10 minutes. Cut into squares while still warm. Yield: 24 bars.

Note: ANZAC stands for the Australian and New Zealand Army Corps - a group of men and women who fought bravely and loyally in World War I and World War II.

138

Caramel Apple Chunks

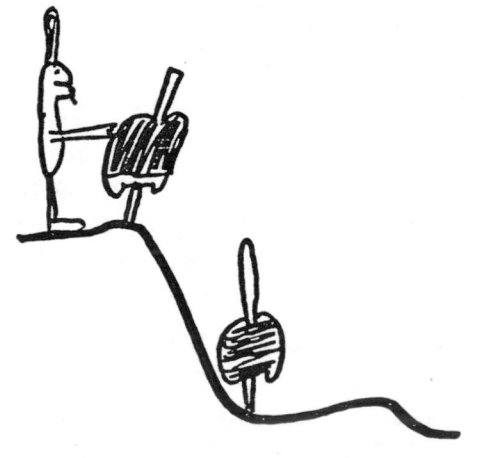

Ingredients

5 medium apples
1 pound (500g) cararmels
2 tablespoons water

Directions

Wash, dry, and cut up the apples into bite-size pieces. Divide and place in individual bowls. In a small saucepan or in the microwave oven, heat and stir the caramels and water. When melted and smooth pour over the apples. Wait until cool before serving. If refrigerated, cararmel will harden quickly. Yield: 6 servings.

139

Chocolate-dipped Bananas

Ingredients
3 firm ripe bananas
1 square unsweetened chocolate
1/4 cup sugar
3 tablespoons warm milk
1/4 teaspoon vanilla extract

Directions
Peel and halve the bananas. Chop chocolate and put in a blender with sugar, milk, and vanilla. Blend until smooth and put in a saucepan to keep warm. Insert a wooden meat skewer into each banana half and store in the freezer for an hour. Pour the chocolate sauce into a small pan. Remove bananas from freezer and dip, one by one, into the chocolate. Serve at once or return to the freezer wrapped in foil. Yield: 6 servings.

Note: *Fruit sauces can be used instead of chocolate sauce. However, they will not adhere to the bananas quite as well.*

140

Fairytale Ambrosia

Ingredients

1 orange
1/2 cantaloupe
Small bunch of grapes
1 banana
1/2 cup shredded coconut

Directions

Peel the orange, cantaloupe and banana. Cut
the fruit into small pieces. Rinse and separate
the grapes. Arrange alternate layers of fruit
and coconut, leaving some coconut for the top.
Pour a little orange juice over the fruit and chill
before serving. Yield: 4 servings.

Note *Ambrosia means <u>the food of the gods</u>
and is used for foods that are delicious or
fragrant.*

141

Red Hot Applesauce Swirl

Ingredients

1 packet plain gelatin
1/2 cup red cinnamon candies
2 1/2 cups boiling water
2 cups unsweetened applesauce
1 tablespoon lemon juice
6 ounces (160g) cream cheese
1/4 cup milk
2 tablespoons mayonnaise

Directions

Dissolve gelatin and cinnamon candies in boiling water. Add applesauce and lemon juice.
Chill until partially set. Pour into a 9 x 9 x 2 inch pan. Blend softened cheese, milk and
mayonnaise until smooth. Spoon cheese mixture on gelatin
mixture and gently swirl through gelatin. Chill until firm.
Yield 6 - 8 servings.

142

Cantaloupe Canoes

Ingredients

1 ripe cantaloupe
Assorted fresh fruits
- apple wedges
- banana slices
- berries in season
- pineapple chunks
- watermelon
- grapes

Directions

Halve the cantaloupe and remove seeds. Scoop out some of the flesh and cut up. Fill cavities with assorted fruits. Poke drinking straws or popsicle sticks through sides of cantaloupe to look like oars. Drizzle plain or vanilla yogurt over top. Yield: 4 servings.

143

Pot of Gold Salad

Ingredients
1 can chunk pineapple
2 bananas, peeled
2 oranges, peeled
1 melon, peeled and balled.
Lettuce leaves, bib or butter

Creamy Pineapple Dressing
Pour pineapple juice into blender. Add 2 tablespoons lemon juice, 1/2 cup cottage cheese, and pinch of salt. Blend until smooth.

Directions
Drain pineapple, saving juice for dressing. Slice bananas and dice oranges. Line 4 plates with lettuce leaves. Arrange fruit on lettuce. Top with Creamy Pineapple dressing. Yield: 4 servings.

Note: Children often don't eat oranges because they find them difficult to peel. Try soaking orange in boiling water first. Cool under cold water and then skin will peel off more easily.

144

Apricot Sticks

Ingredients

1 pound (500g) dried apricots
1 orange
11/2 cups sugar
3/4 cup chopped pecans (optional)
Powdered sugar

Directions

Put the dried apricots and cut up orange (peeling and all) in food chopper or food processor. Dissolve the sugar with a little water in a small saucepan. Add apricot mixture and boil for 10 minutes stirring constantly. Remove from heat. Add the finely chopped pecans if desired. Mix well. Drop by spoonfuls in powdered sugar. Roll into sticks. Store in an airtight container and serve as snacks or candy. Yield: Varies.

Note: *Dried fruits always make excellent candy substitutes. Unfortunately, they are often more expensive. Friends of ours have invested in a food dehydrator and have homemade dried fruits on hand year-round for their kids.*

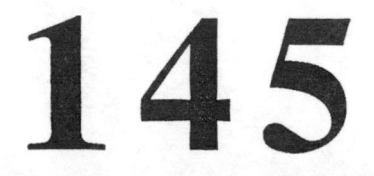

145

Cottage Cheese and Melon Slices

Ingredients
1   8 ounce (250g) carton low fat cottage cheese
1   cup cantaloupe slices
1   cup honey-dew melon slices
1   cup watermelon slices
1/4 cup cinnamon sugar

Directions
This fresh fruit dish is very easy to prepare. Once the fruit is sliced and cut up into bite-sized pieces, it is placed in individual serving bowls. Add 1 or 2 scoops of cottage cheese and sprinkle cinnamon sugar on top. Yield: 4 servings.

Note: *Before leaving for picnic, place cut fruit in a sealed plastic bag. Put fruit and carton of cottage cheese in the cooler. Serve fruit and cottage cheese in plastic cups and eat with plastic forks or spoons. Remember to dispose of all containers and plastic cutlery in the trash containers provided at the picnic site (or bring them all home with you). Smokey the Bear will be pleased!*

146

Candy Apples

Ingredients

5 firm fresh apples
2 cups sugar
2/3 cup light corn syrup
1 cup water
Red vegetable coloring
5 skewers or popsicle sticks

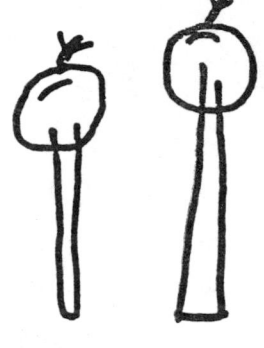

Directions

Wash, dry, and insert a skewer in the stem end of the apples. Grease a cookie tray or piece of aluminum foil. In a saucepan combine sugar, syrup, and water. Bring to a boil. Cook covered 3 minutes. Uncover and cook without stirring to the brittle stage when tested in a cup of ice-cold water. Add a few drops of red coloring. Keep candy warm in a double boiler. Dip in the apples on skewers. Place them skewers up, on the greased tray or foil to harden. If desired, dip apples in a bowl of chopped nuts, crushed dry cereal, sprinkles, or coconut. Eat when completely hardened. Store wrapped in well-greased wax paper or foil.
Yield: 5 candy apples.

147

We Three Fruit Slurpy

Ingredients
3 bananas
3 lemons
3 oranges
1 cup sugar
3 cups water

Directions
Squeeze the juice from the lemons and oranges. Peel and mash the bananas. Combine the fruits with the sugar and water. Mix well. Pour into freezer trays and freeze. Remove from trays once or twice and beat well. Return to freezer. When icy, but not completely frozen, scoop into tall glasses. Yield: 4 - 6.

Note: *These slurpies are good on a hot day and take much longer to drink than a regular fruit cooler. Ripe fruit other than bananas can be used and the sugar can be adjusted to taste.*

148

Ghosts and goblins
pumpkins too
steaming pots
of witches brew

Holidays

Scary music
tricks and treats
cheerful chatter
bags of sweets

Haunted houses
shrieks of fright
it's Halloween
Our favorite night!

Queen of Hearts Tarts

Ingredients

2 cups unbleached flour
4 tablespoons margarine
4 tablespoons lard
Pinch of salt
2 1/2 tablespoons water
Natural jam

Directions

Preheat oven to 425°F (180°C). Sift flour and salt into bowl. Cut the butter and lard into the flour with tips of fingers, making fine crumbs. Sprinkle water over the mixture and mix to a smooth, stiff dough. Dust working surface with flour and roll out pastry about 1/4 inch thick. Cut rounds a bit larger than the muffin tins. Press each round into tin. Put jam on each round. Sprinkle a thin layer of water on jam. Bake 10 to 15 minutes. Yield: 12 to 15 tarts.

Mealtime Question: Who do you love and why?

149

St. Patrick's Popcorn Balls

Ingredients

2 cups white sugar
1/4 teaspoon cream of tartar
1/2 cup boiling water
1 tablespoon butter
1/2 teaspoon baking soda
2 pans popcorn
Green gum drops, cut in small pieces

Directions

Put sugar, cream of tartar and water in a saucepan to boil. Put a lid on pan and boil for 5 minutes. Take lid off and continue boiling until the mixture becomes yellowish. Add butter and soda. Mix gum drops with popcorn. Pour cararmel mixture over the top of popcorn mixture. Mix together with spoon. When cool, shape into balls with hands. Try making a three leaf clover or a leprechaun. Yield: 24 balls.

150

Mealtime Question: *What is the luckiest thing that ever happened to you?*

Easter Egg Braid

Directions

Combine first 3 ingredients. Measure flour and salt into a bowl. Make a well and add the rest of the ingredients except for last three eggs. Beat well until a ball of dough is formed, then turn out onto a floured board and knead for 10 minutes until smooth and elastic. Place in a greased bowl, cover, and allow to rise until doubled in bulk (about one hour). Punch down and divide dough into two sections. Cut each section of dough into 3 parts and roll between hands into long cylinders. With the three ropes of dough lying side by side start to braid loosely inserting raw decorated eggs every now and then. Finish the ends by tucking them under. Repeat for the second loaf. Cover and let rise until almost doubled in bulk. Brush tops with 1 egg yolk diluted with 1 tablespoon milk. Bake 15 minutes in a 400°F (200°C) oven. Reduce heat to 375°F (190°C) and bake for 45 minutes. Yield: 10 servings.

Ingredients

2 packages active dry yeast
1 teaspoon sugar
1/4 cup warm water
6 cups unbleached flour
1 tablespoon salt
2 cups warm water
3 beaten eggs
1/4 cup vegetable oil
3 tablespoons sugar
8 raw decorated eggs
1 egg yolk
1 tablespoon milk

151

Chocolate Bunnies

Ingredients

1/2 cup butterscotch pieces
1/2 cup chocolate pieces
1/4 cup light corn syrup
2 tablespoons margarine
3 cups crisp rice cereal
Decorations: raisins, coconut,
colored candies, dried fruit, etc.

Directions

Line a baking sheet with waxed paper. Grease top of paper. In a
large heavy saucepan heat butterscotch, chocolate, corn syrup, and
margarine until melted, stirring constantly. Remove from heat and
stir in cereal. Let cool about 15 minutes or until warm to touch. Dip
hands in cold water before shaping cereal mixture into bunnies.
Bunnies can be shaped standing up or lying flat. Decorate
accordingly. Chill before serving. Yield: 12 servings.

152

Mother's Day Souffle

Ingredients
1 loaf natural white bread
2 cups grated cheese
Ham or bacon bits to taste
12 eggs
1/2 cup milk
Seasonings if desired

Directions
This Mother's Day the idea is not only to give mother breakfast in bed, but also to feed the rest of the family so she can stay in bed! This dish can be prepared the night before and placed in the refrigerator. Cut crusts off of bread. Grease a 9x13 inch pan. Place one layer of bread on bottom of pan. Top with cheese and meat. As if making a sandwich, put remaining bread on top. Mix eggs, milk, and any seasoning in a bowl. Pour over top. When ready to bake, put into a preheated 350°F (180°C) oven for 1 hour, or until top is puffy and brown. Serve with fruit salad. You can add other ingredients in-between bread, be creative and experiment! Yield: 8 to 10 servings.

153

Dad's Favorite Brownies

Ingredients

2 ounces (50g)
    semi-sweet chocolate
1/3 cup butter
1/2 cup walnuts
2/3 cup unbleached flour
1/2 teaspoon baking powder
3/4 cup sugar
2 eggs, beaten
1/2 teaspoon vanilla extract

Directions

Preheat oven to 350°F (180°C). Grease an 8-inch square cake pan. Put chocolate pieces and butter into a saucepan and melt over very low heat. Put sugar, eggs, vanilla and walnuts in a bowl. Beat until smooth. Add flour and mix. Add chocolate mixture and beat until smooth.   Pour the batter into the pan and bake for 30 minutes. Cool in pan and cut into squares.   Pack brownies in a plastic bag and ask Dad to go on a hike with you. Today is the day to tell him how special he is! Yield: 24 cookies.

154

Fourth of July Fruit Plate

Ingredients
2 cups frozen whipped topping, thawed
2 cups natural lowfat vanilla yogurt
1/2 teaspoon nutmeg
1/2 teaspoon vanilla
1 watermelon, cut into 3/4 inch strips
6 cups blueberries

Directions
Combine whipped topping, yogurt, nutmeg, and vanilla.
Refrigerate until serving time. Cut watermelon slices into
triangular wedges. Place bowl of dip in the middle of a large plate.
Arrange the blueberries around the bowl. Place the watermelon
wedges tips out, on edge of plate to create a star effect.
Yield: 6 to 8 servings.

*Note: Ants are allergic to white chalk. To keep them away from
food, draw lines along the edges of the picnic table with chalk.*

155

Caramel Apple Bobs

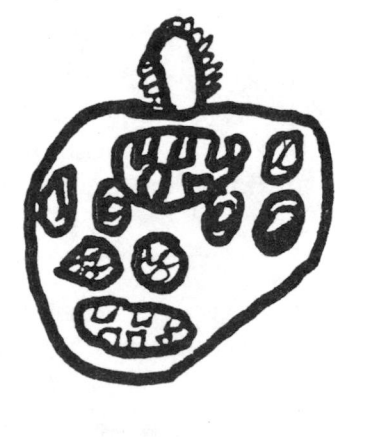

Ingredients
Bag of caramels, unwrapped
6 apples cut into small pieces

Directions
Heat caramels over low heat.
Add 1 or 2 tablespoons water
to thin to desired consistency.
Pour over cut apples and eat!
Yield: 4 to 6 servings.

Note: *Have children play a bobbing-for-apples game before you cut up the apples for dessert. Get a big tub of water and put the apples in it. Tie child's hands behind their backs and have them bob for the apples in the water, trying to pick up apples with their teeth. Make sure you are close by to supervise!*

156

Thanksgiving Muffins

Ingredients

1 1/2 cups unbleached flour
1 cup yellow cornmeal
1/4 cup sugar
2 teaspoons baking powder

1 cup buttermilk
1/4 cup vegetable oil
1 egg, beaten
1 tablespoon grated orange peel
1 cup fresh or frozen cranberries

Directions

Preheat oven to 400°F (200°C). In a medium bowl combine the flour, cornmeal, sugar, baking powder and salt. Make a hole in the middle of the dry ingredients and add the buttermilk, oil, egg, and orange peel. Stir until just moistened. Gently fold in the cranberries. Spoon the batter into paper muffin cups or directly into greased and floured muffin pans, filling 3/4 full. Bake 20 to 25 minutes or until golden brown on top. Yield: 24 muffins.

Note: *Researchers find that given a choice between food that is good for them or food that just tastes good, children will opt for foods that taste sweet. Infants and toddlers do not know instinctively what foods are the best for them so they need lots of nutrition guidance.*

157

Thanksgiving Pudding

Ingredients
2/3 cup minute rice
1 cup apple juice
1/4 teaspoon cinnamon
1/2 cup packed brown sugar
1/4 cup raisins
1 cup diced apples
1 tablespoon butter
2 egg whites
3 tablespoons white sugar

Directions
Mix first 6 ingredients in sauce pan. Bring to a boil and simmer 5 to 10 minutes, until liquid disappears. Add butter. Put into dessert dishes. To make the meringue topping beat 2 egg whites until stiff. Add 3 tablespoons sugar and beat. Top each pudding with meringue and place under the broiler until light brown. Eat hot or cold.
Yield: 4 servings.

158

Activity: While you prepare this dish, tell your child how the pilgrims sailed across the sea to live in America.....

Holiday French Toast

Ingredients

6 slices bread (any kind, cut in half)
1/2 cup eggnog
1 cup corn flakes
2 tablespoons cooking oil for frying
Pure maple syrup or honey

Directions

Pour oil into skillet over medium heat. Dip the pieces of bread into the eggnog on both sides. Roll the dipped bread in the cornflakes and fry for one to two minutes on each side. Cover with syrup or honey and serve warm.
Yield: 4 servings.

159

Mealtime Question: *Tell me about last Christmas; what were your favorite moments?*

Menorah Pineapple Salad

Ingredients

5 bananas
9 pineapple rings
9 cherries
2 cups cottage cheese
Lettuce leaves

Directions

Decorate plate with pretty lettuce leaves Place pineapple on top of the leaves. Place a scoop of cottage cheese in the center of each pineapple ring. Cut bananas in half and stick into the cottage cheese, to look like a candle. Place a cherry on top, to represent the flame. Yield: 8 servings.

Activity: Tonight take a few minutes to do something special before bed. Read a story, talk about your day, and hug each other.

160

Santa Claus Eggs

Ingredients
Hard boiled eggs
 (1/2 egg for each serving plus 1 extra)
1 large tomato
Whole cloves, 2 for each 1/2 egg
Lettuce leaves

Directions
Peel eggs. Cut peeled eggs in half lengthwise and set them yolkside up on wax paper. Remove yolk from the extra egg and slice its white into sections about 1/4 inch thick. From these slices, cut Santa's mustache, and a small triangle for the tip of Santa's hat. To make Santa's hat and nose, wash and cut the tomato in half. With spoon, carefully scoop out all pulp onto wax paper. For hat cut triangles out of the tomato skin about 1 1/2 inches on each side. For nose, cut a 3/8 inch oval. To attach hat make a 1/2 inch deep slit in the widest end of the egg and fit tomato in it. Place egg white triange on top of hat. Stick cloves into yolk for eyes (don't eat cloves). Add mustache and place on lettuce leaves.

161

Candy Canes

Ingredients

1 cup butter or margarine
1 cup sugar
3 eggs
1 teaspoon vanilla
3 cups unbleached white flour
1 teaspoon baking powder
Red vegetable food coloring

Directions

Preheat oven to 350°F (180°C). Beat butter and sugar in large bowl. Add eggs and vanilla. Sift in baking powder, salt, and flour. Mix with hands until pliable. Divide dough into two balls. Set one ball on waxed paper. Add food coloring to the other ball; knead. Make 7 inch long ropes by rubbing hand over top of small ball of dough. Pinch white and red dough together at top and twist   Place on greased cookie sheet, shaping the rope like a candy cane. Bake for 8 to 12 minutes. Yield: 12 to 18 candy canes.

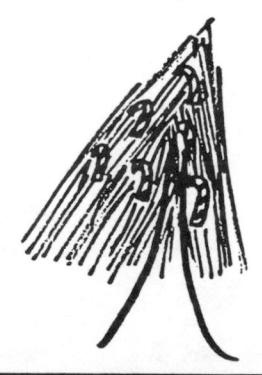

162

Christmas Cookies

Ingredients
1 cup butter or margarine
1 cup sugar or 3/4 cup honey
2 eggs
1 teaspoon vanilla extract
2 3/4 cups unbleached flour
1 teaspoon baking powder
1 teaspoon salt
Glaze
1 cup powdered sugar
2 tablespoons milk

Directions
Preheat oven to 350°F (180°C). Beat together butter and sugar. Add eggs and vanilla extract and beat well. Slowly add flour, baking powder and salt. Dough should form a ball and feel dry. Roll 1/3 of dough on a floured surface to 1/4 inch thickness. Use favorite cookie cutters to cut shapes. Top with sugar sprinkles, raisins, carob chips, or glaze when cool. Yield: 24 cookies.

163

Pineapple Wreath

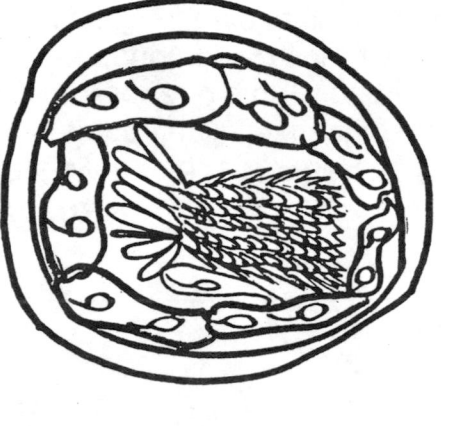

Ingredients

6 pineapple slices
6 lettuce leaves
Small bunch of watercress
10   cherries, raspberries, or strawberries
8 ounces (225g) cream cheese
   or kefir cheese
4 tablespoons natural mayonnaise
1/4 cup powdered sugar

Directions

Arrange lettuce leaves on plate. Place pineapple around
plate in the shape of a wreath. Put watercress on top of
pineapple. Put berries on top of watercress. Mix cheese
with mayonnaise until smooth. Fill the center of the
pineapple ring with cheese mixture and chill. Sprinkle with
sugar and serve. Yield: 6 servings.

164

Nothing smells better
on a cold autumn day
than a casserole baking
in a pot made of clay.

Meats

Delicious main dishes
prepared with great care
Rich, spicy aromas
encircle the air.

Warm fires burning
Gathered 'round the rug
Families together
so cozy and snug!

My Mini-Meat Pies

Ingredients
Cheese Pastry
1/2 pound lean ground beef
1 small onion, chopped
1/2 teaspoon salt
1/4 teaspoon marjoram
1 teaspoon dried parsley
1 tablespoon dry bread crumbs

Cheese Pastry
1 cup margarine
1 cup cream cheese or kefir cheese
2 cups whole-wheat flour
1 tablespoon honey
1/4 teaspoon salt

Cream margarine, honey, and cream cheese together until smooth and creamy. Sift together remaining ingredients. Work into creamed mixture with a wooden spoon until completely blended. Form into a ball and chill several hours.

Directions
Preheat oven to 425°F (215°C). In a frying pan, brown meat with onion. Add remaining ingredients. Allow to cool while rolling pastry to about 1/8" thickness. Cut rolled pastry into 4" squares; place about 1 tablespoon filling on each. Fold in half diagonally and press edges with fork to seal. Place on lightly greased cookie sheets and bake 15 minutes. Yield: 12 mini pies.

165

Middle Eastern Lamb

Ingredients
1 tablespoon vegetable oil
2 pounds (1k) lamb
Salt and pepper
1/2 onion, minced
2 1/2 cups chicken stock
1 cup dried figs
1 1/4 cups uncooked rice
1 1/2 teaspoons allspice
1/2 teaspoon cinnamon

Directions
Heat the oil in a large heavy saucepan. Sprinkle the lamb pieces with salt and pepper and brown them in the oil, about 5 minutes. Drain excess oil. Add the onion and cook until soft. Add the stock and bring to a boil. Reduce the heat and simmer covered, for 20 minutes. Remove the stems from the figs and cut in half. Stir the rice, spices, and figs into the lamb mixture. Cover and simmer until rice is tender, about 15 minutes. Remove from heat and let sit for about 10 minutes. Serve with sauteed vegetables or a green salad and couscous. Yield: 8 servings.

166

Hale and Hearty Brisket

Ingredients
4 - 5 pound (2k) beef brisket
1 package onion soup mix
1 package mushroom gravy mix
1 1/2 cups water
1 onion, sliced
4 small potatoes, peeled and cubed
3 carrots, peeled and cubed.

Directions
Place all ingredients in a slow-cooker and cover and bake on high for 5 -6 hours. *Or* preheat oven to 350°F (180°C) and bake covered for 4 - 5 hours. Transfer meat to serving platter and slice. To serve, spoon gravy and vegetables over meat. Accompany meal with chunks of fresh sourdough bread.
Yield: 6 servings.

167

Beef Strogonoff

Ingredients

1 pound (500g) minute steak, cut in strips
1 tablespoon onion flakes
1 package chicken soup mix
1/2 teaspoon garlic powder
4 tablespoons ketchup

1 teaspoon Worcestershire sauce
1/2 cup sliced mushrooms
1/2 cup sour cream
1 cup cooked noodles

Directions

Saute strips of steak in greased frying pan until brown. Add 2 cups hot water, onion flakes, soup mix, garlic, ketchup, and Worcestershire sauce. Mix well and let simmer for 10 minutes. Stir in mushrooms and milk. Lastly, blend in sour cream. Heat through. Serve over noodles.

168

Chili

Ingredients
1 pound lean ground beef
1 packet chili mix
2 cans stewed tomatoes
1 can pinto beans, drained
1 onion, chopped
1 packet (4 ounces) unsalted crackers

Directions
Brown the ground beef in a frying pan. Drain off any excess fat. Sprinkle the chili mix over the meat and stir to blend with a cup of water. Add the stewed tomatoes. Cover and simmer for 20 minutes. Stir in the beans and cook until heated through. Serve the chili in bowls or ramekins with the chopped onion and crackers on the side. Yield: 6 servings.

Note: *Children are generally cautious when it comes to hot foods. You may want to taste-test the chili before serving it. To be on the safe side, try using only 1/2 the packet of chili mix.*

169

Shepherd's Pie

Ingredients

1 pound (500g) ground beef
1 each onion and carrot
2 cups beef broth or bouillon
Salt and pepper to taste
2 cups cooked potatoes
1 tablespoon butter or margarine
1/4 cup milk
4 slices cheddar cheese

Directions

Preheat oven to 350°F (180°C). Brown ground beef and drain off the fat. Add chopped onion diced carrot, broth, salt, and pepper. Simmer for 20 minutes or until meat is tender. Thicken with 2 tablespoons cornstarch dissolved in 1/4 cup water. Stir until smooth and bubbling.

Pour into a deep baking dish. Mash potatoes with butter and milk. Spread slices of cheese over meat mixture then pile potatoes on top, spreading to touch sides of dish. Bake for 15 minutes or until peaks of potatoes are golden brown. Cool slightly before serving. Yield: 6 servings.

170

Hot Dog Enchiladas

Ingredients

2 cans chili, without beans
1 teaspoon onion, minced
1 package hot dogs
1 package flour tortillas
1 8 ounce (250g) can tomato sauce
1 small can green peppers, chopped
1 cup cheddar cheese, grated

Directions

Preheat oven to 350°F (180°C). Mix together the chili and minced onion. Place a hot dog in the center of each tortilla and cover each one with 2 tablespoons of the chili mixture. Roll up and place totillas side by side in a greased baking dish seam side down. Combine the remaining chili mixture with the tomato sauce and peppers. Pour over the tortillas and place in the oven uncovered, for 20 minutes. Remove from oven and sprinkle the grated cheese on top. Return to oven for 15 minutes. Cool and serve with Spanish rice and a salad. Yield: 10 - 12.

171

Ground Beef Stew

Ingredients
1 pound (500g) lean ground beef
2 carrots, peeled and sliced
1 onion, peeled and chopped
2 cups water or beef bouillon
1 tablespoon steak sauce
2 tablespoons cornstarch
1/2 cup frozen or fresh peas

Directions
Brown the ground beef in a frying pan or dutch oven. Drain off excess fat. Add carrots, onion, steak sauce, and water or bouillon. Let simmer for 30 minutes. Mix cornstarch with 1/4 cup water. Slowly pour into beef mixture stirring constantly. When mixture thickens, add peas and simmer for 5 minutes. Serve with mashed potatoes. Yield: 4 servings.

Note: This is a favorite dish of New Zealand and Australian children and they call it "mince" because the beef was put through a meat grinder and came out minced.

172

Sloppy Joannas

Ingredients

1 onion, chopped
1 tablespoon vegetable oil
11/2 pounds (750g) ground beef
2 tablespoon ketchup
2 cans tomato sauce
4 hamburger buns

Directions

Heat oil in frypan or electric skillet. Add chopped onion and cook until transparent. Add the ground beef and cook, stirring often, until brown and crumbly. Drain off excess fat. Add catsup and tomato sauce and simmer mixture for 10 minutes. Meanwhile, split and toast the hamburger buns. To serve, spoon the hamburger mixture over the bun halves. Garnish the child's plate with carrot sticks and potato chips. Yield: 4 servings.

Note: Children are not born tidy. However, if parents keep the rest of the house neat and clean, and if they allow the child to experience the natural consequences of untidiness, the child will eventually learn to change her ways.

173

Sneaky Meat Loaf

Ingredients

1 pound (550g) lean ground beef
1 cup uncooked oats
1 pound (500g) spaghetti sauce
1/2 chopped onion
1/3 cup parmesan cheese
1 egg

1 tablespoon Worcestershire sauce
1/2 cup shredded mozzarella cheese
1/2 cup of any of the following: sliced mushrooms, shredded zucchini, grated cheese, mashed potatoes, grated carrots, cooked vegetables, frozen peas, sliced tomatoes, cold macaroni cheese, or broken potato chips.

Directions

Preheat oven to 350°F (180°C). Grease a deep 8-inch round baking pan. Combine ground beef, oats, 3/4 cup spaghetti sauce, onion, parmesan cheese, egg, and Worcestershire sauce. Mix well. Halve mixture and shape into two circular patties, about 7 inches in diameter. Place stuffing choice on top of one patty. Cover with the other patty and seal by pinching sides together. Place into pan. Bake 40 to 45 minutes. Cover with remaining spaghetti sauce and top with mozzarella cheese. Return to oven to melt cheese. Serve with baked potatoes and a vegetables. Yield: 6 servings.

174

Very Easy Beef Stew

Ingredients

1 to 1 1/2 pounds cubed beef stew meat
3 tablespoons flour
2 tablespoons vegetable oil
3 cups water
1 packet beef stew or gravy seasoning mix
4 potatoes, scrubbed and cut up
4 carrots, peeled and sliced
2 onions, peeled and quartered.
10–ounce (275g) packet of frozen peas

Directions

Coat the stew meat with flour and then brown in a Dutch oven in the heated oil. Add the water and seasoning mix. Stir well and bring to a boil. Reduce heat and simmer, covered, 1 1/2 hours. Add all the vegetables except the peas. Cover and simmer 1 hour or until vegetables are tender. Add the package of peas during last 5 minutes. Stir often while stew is cooking. This stew can also be prepared in a crockpot. Cook 6 to 8 hours. Yield: 6 - 8 servings.

175

Pork Chops and Apple Sauce

Ingredients

3/4 cup apple juice
1/2 teaspoon salt
1/2 teaspoon ground cloves
4 thick pork chops
1 tablespoon vegetable oil
1 cup applesauce

Directions

Prepare marinade by combining apple juice, salt, and cloves In a shallow dish. Add pork chops, turning to coat. Chill covered, for several hours. Preheat oven to 350°F (180°C). Remove chops and brown in oil in frying pan. Place chops in baking dish and brush with marinade. Bake for 1 hour. Transfer to serving platters and top each chop with the apple sauce. Yield: 4 servings.

17

Barbecued Baby Ribs

Ingredients
1 cup barbecue sauce
1/2 cup soy sauce
1 cup ketchup
1 onion, minced
1 tablespoon honey
2 pounds (1k) baby back ribs

Directions
Make barbecue sauce by combining all the ingredients except ribs. Marinate ribs in sauce overnight. To cook, preheat oven to 300°F (150°C). Place ribs and sauce in an uncovered casserole dish and bake for 1 hour or until meat separates from bones. Serve warm with a green salad and baked potatoes.

Note: *Barbecue ribs are messy and delicious. The term barbecue comes from the French "de barbe a queue" which means from beard to tail. Back in the old days, whole animals, including goats, were roasted on a spit over an open fire.*

177

Teriyaki Lamb Chops

Ingredients
4 lamb shoulder chops, about 3/4 inch thick
1/2 cup soy sauce
2 tablespoons brown sugar
1/2 teaspoon each ginger and garlic powder
1/4 cup pineapple juice

Directions
Make a marinade by mixing together thoroughly all the ingredients except the chops. Trim the fat off the chops and add to marinade. Turn to coat both sides then store covered, in the refrigerator overnight. Turn again once or twice. Broil on outdoor grill 4 inches from coals for about 12 minutes per side. Serve with a green salad and fluffy rice. Yield: 4 servings.

Note: You can make your own delicious teriyaki sauce by mixing together and heating 1/2 cup beef stock, 3 tablespoons each soy sauce, lemon juice, dry sherry, and honey. Stir in 1/2 teaspoon each ground ginger and garlic powder. Serve warm or cold.

178

Crockpot Lamb and Wild Rice

Ingredients

1 pound lamb stew meat, cubed
2 tablespoons flour
1/2 teaspoon seasoned salt
2 tablespoons vegetable oil
2 cups assorted vegetables, cut up
2 cups broth or bouillon
1/2 cup wild rice

Directions

Toss lamb in flour and salt and brown in heated oil. Put in crockpot along with vegetables and rice. Pour broth over the top. Cook covered on low for about 6 hours. Stir once or twice. Serve with French bread. Yield: 4 servings.

Note: *Wild rice is just what its name suggests. It comes from a grass that grows wild in the midwest and northern United States. it is actually more closely related to wheat than it is to rice. Rinse it well before using.*

179

Veal Roll-ups

Ingredients
1 pound (500g) veal cutlets
Salt and pepper to taste
1/2 cup celery, finely chopped
1/2 cup carrots, grated
1 tablespoon minced parsley
1/2 cup corn
1 1/2 cups beef bouillon

Directions
Preheat oven to 350°F (180°C). Cut veal into 4 thin slices. Season with salt and pepper. In a small bowl, combine the celery, carrots, parsley, and corn. Spoon 1/4 of the vegetables onto each veal slice. Roll up and secure with a toothpick. Place roll-ups in baking dish and bake for 30 minutes or until golden brown. Pour the beef bouillon over the the roll-ups and bake another 30 minutes or until veal is tender. Serve with buttered noodles or new potatoes. Yield: 4 servings.

Note: *Eating for children should be a relaxing experience and also an important part of their day. For them, eating is as serious as playing - and it can be just as creative and absorbing.*

180

Weiner Schnitzel

Ingredients

1 pound (500g) veal cutlets
1 egg, beaten
2 tablespoons milk
1/2 cup unbleached flour
Salt and pepper to taste
1 cup breadcrumbs
2 tablespoons butter or vegetable oil

Directions

Pound veal cutlets to about 1/4 inch thick. Beat egg and milk together and pour into shallow bowl. Toss flour with salt and pepper and spread on waxed paper. Spread breadcrumbs on waxed paper too. Heat butter or oil in frying pan. Coat cutlet with flour, then egg mixture and finally breadcrumbs. Let stand for 10 minutes. Saute cutlets in frying pan for 2 minutes on each side. Turn again and cook for 10 minutes or until meat is tender. Serve garnished with lemon slices. Yield: 4 servings.

181

ON THE GO→

Rain on my campfire
Rain on my tent
Rain on my sandwich
all soggy and bent

Six days of rain
no sign of the sun
Who ever said that
camping was fun????

Cheddar Cheese Cookies

Ingredients

3/4 cup flour
2/3 cup margarine
1/3 cup firmly packed brown sugar
1 teaspoon vanilla
1 egg
1/2 teaspoon cinnamon
1/2 teaspoon baking powder

1/2 teaspoon salt
1 1/2 cups oatmeal
1 cup shredded cheddar cheese
3/4 cup raisins
1 cup peeled chopped apple

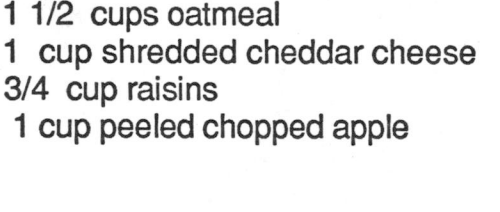

Directions

Preheat oven to 375°F (190°C). Combine flour, margarine, sugar, vanilla, egg, cinnamon, baking powder, and salt. Mix well. Add oatmeal, cheese, and raisins; mix well. Stir in apple. Drop by tablespoons onto ungreased cookie sheet. Bake 15 minutes or until golden brown. Yield: 24 cookies.

182

Tiny Tuna Souffle

Ingredients

7 ounces (200g) tuna packed in water
6 tablespoons plain yogurt
1/4 apple, chopped
1 tablespoon lemon juice
1 tablespoon honey
2 teaspoons soy sauce
1 teaspoon mustard
4 tablespoons grated cheddar cheese
1 cup cooked brown or white rice
2 egg whites

Directions

Preheat oven to 375°F (180°C). In a large bowl, combine all the
ingredients except egg whites and blend. In another bowl beat
egg whites until stiff peaks form. Fold eggs into tuna mixture.
Grease muffin tins and fill with the tuna mixture. Bake 45 minutes.
Chill and eat. Yield: 12 servings.

183

Hideout Crunchies

Ingredients
1/3 cup light corn syrup
1/3 cup peanut butter
2 tablespoons sugar
1 1/2 cups puffed wheat or corn
1 cup popcorn
1/2 cup Spanish peanuts or raisins

Directions
Heat syrup, peanut butter, and sugar in a large microwave bowl at HIGH until mixture comes to a boil, for 2 minutes. Stir in remaining ingredients. Cool slightly. Wet hands with cold water and shape into small balls about the size of golf balls. Store wrapped in wax paper. Yield: 20 - 30 crunchy balls.

Note: To cook on the range-top, bring first 3 ingredients to a full boil stirring constantly. Pour over remaining ingredients in a large bowl. Cool and shape as directed above.

184

I'm Late Omelet

Ingredients

10" pastry shell pre-baked in 400°F (205°C)
    oven for 5 minutes and cooled.
1 cup chicken or vegetable stock
1 cup water
1/2 cup unbleached flour
1/4 cup soft margarine

1 cup grated cheese
5 eggs, slightly beaten
1/4 teaspoon salt
1/4 teaspoon dry mustard
1/4 teaspoon black pepper

Directions

Preheat the oven to 400°F (205°C). In a saucepan stir the liquids
into the flour until smooth. Bring to a boil, cook, and stir until thick.
Remove from heat. Add margarine and stir until blended. Add
remaining ingredients, pour into pie shell, and bake for 30
minutes. Cut into wedges, eat, or cool and put omelet into a bag
for breakfast or lunch on the go! Yield: 8 servings.

185

Vegetable Flat Bread

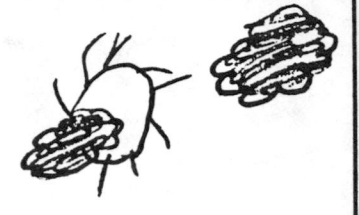

Ingredients
1 cup washed, peeled, grated, carrots
1 cup washed peeled, grated, zuchinni
8 tablespoons grated parmesan cheese
2 eggs, beaten
1/4 cup olive oil
2 tablespoons chopped parsley
1 teaspoon oregano
1 tablespoon soy sauce

Directions
Preheat oven to 350°F (180°C). Place all of the ingredients in a
large bowl and stir well. Grease a 9-inch square pan. Spread the
mixture into pan and bake for 20 to 25 minutes, until light brown.
Cut when cool and pack for that special picnic or car trip.
Yield: 12 servings.

186

Potato Cheese Saucers

Ingredients

1 cup unbleached flour
1/2 teaspoon salt
3 teaspoons baking powder
1/4 cup butter or margarine
1/3 cup sugar
1/2 cup mashed potatoes
4 tablespoons milk, to mix
Cheese slices
Mustard

Directions

Preheat oven to 425°F (220°C). Sift flour, salt and baking powder into bowl. Rub in the butter until the mixture becomes crumbly. Stir in sugar and mashed potatoes. Add the milk and mix to a soft, but not sticky, dough. Knead the dough lightly on a floured surface. Roll out to 1/2" thickness. Using a shaped cookie cutter, cut dough and place on a greased cookie sheet. Bake for 12 to 15 minutes. Cool slightly and slice, put cheese and mustard in between and eat! Yield: 8 to 12 servings.

187

Naturally Soft Pretzels

Directions

In a large bowl, mix the first 7 ingredients very well. Cover with a clean, damp towel and set in a warm place to rise for 1 hour. Remove mixture from warm place and stir. Add the baking soda, yogurt and the additional flour. Set aside until well risen. Knead down. Divide the dough into 10 equal pieces. Roll a piece into a long snake, about 20 inches by 1/2 inch, then twist into an overhand knot or pretzel shape. Repeat until all pretzels are twisted. Simmer a few inches of water in the bottom of a wide pot. Lightly grease baking sheet. Place raw pretzels into the barely simmering water for a few seconds. Drain , then lay on a greased baking sheet. Sprinkle tops of pretzels with optional coatings; poppy seeds, Parmesan cheese, etc. Starting in a cold oven, bake at 375°F (190°C) for 20 to 30 minutes, until brown.

Ingredients

1   teaspoon salt
1   tablespoon active dry yeast
1   cup hot tap water
1/3 cup instant milk powder
1/4 cup unsaturated vegetable oil
2   tablespoons honey
1 1/2 cups whole wheat flour
1   teaspoon baking soda
1/2 cup natural yogurt
1 1/2 cups whole wheat flour
Yield: 12 pretzels.

188

Chewy Fruit Bars

Ingredients
1/2 cup margarine
3/4 cup packed brown sugar
1/2 cup molasses
1 egg
1 teaspoon cinnamon
1/4 teaspoon ground ginger
1/2 teaspoon baking soda
1 cup unbleached flour
1 1/2 cups chopped dried
    fruit (apricots, apples, etc.)

Directions
Preheat oven to 350°F (180°C). In a large bowl beat margarine, sugar, and molasses until smooth. Add egg. Stir in spices and soda. Stir in flour and dried fruit until evenly moist. Spread dough in a greased 10 x 15 inch baking pan. Bake for 25 minutes. Yield: 12 bars.

189

Cheese and Tomato Quiche

Ingredients

1 nine-inch pie shell
2 tomatoes, seeded and chopped
1 teaspoon salt
3/4 cup grated Swiss cheese
1 cup whole milk
3 large eggs

Directions

Preheat oven to 375°F (190°C). Sprinkle cheese and tomatoes on bottom of pie crust. Mix eggs, cream, and salt together. Pour over cheese and tomatoes. Bake 45 minutes or until center is firm and top browned and puffed. Chill. Wrap up and put in tomorrow's lunch! Yield: 8 servings.

Activity: Give your child a large piece of white butcher paper. Have them trace their plate, glass, fork, spoon etc. Now let them eat their meal on the imaginary place setting.

190

Grandma's Granola

Ingredients

2 1/2 cups uncooked oats
1/2 cup coconut
1/2 cup almonds or seeds
     (omit for children under 3)
1/2 cup bran or grapenuts
1/2 cup margarine
1/2 cup honey
1/2 cup raisins or dates

Directions

Mix first four ingredients. Melt margarine and honey, and stir into dry ingredients. Spread evenly on cookie tray. Bake at 300°F (150°C) stirring often, for 20 minutes. When finished cooking stir in raisins. Cool before storing in airtight jar or container. Yield: 12 servings.

Note: *Sometimes honey becomes crystallized if it is stored for a while. Set it in hot water or briefly microwave to make it a liquid.*

191

Cheesey Chocolate Cupcakes

Ingredients

1 1/2 cups unbleached flour
1 cup sugar
1/4 cup cocoa or carob powder
1 teaspoon baking soda
1/2 cup oil
1 teaspoon vinegar
1 teaspoon vanilla
1 cup water
8 ounces (225 g) cream cheese
1 egg
1/3 cup sugar
dash salt

Directions

This recipe is for children over three years.
Preheat oven to 350°F (180°C). Place muffin cups in muffin tin. Combine first 8 ingredients and beat well. Fill tins 1/2 full with chocolate mixture. Combine cheese, egg, and sugar in a small bowl and beat well. Drop 1 tablespoon of cheese mixture in each cupcake. Bake for 20 minutes. Yield 12 to 15 cupcakes.

192

Bread Sticks

Ingredients

4 cups wheat, rye, or white flour
1 package dried yeast
1 teaspoon salt
3 tablespoons oil
1 1/4 cups milk

Directions

Place 3 cups flour into a large bowl. Add the yeast to 3 tablespoons warm water and let sit until foamy. Add yeast, salt, oil, and milk to the flour. Knead energetically for 10 minutes (break up the dough and let little hands knead also!). Dough should be smooth and elastic. Put in a warm place to rise for 1 1/2 hours. Preheat oven to 450°F (230°C). Divide dough into pieces and roll into long thin sticks with floured hands. Cut the sticks into 10 inch (25cm) lengths. Put on oiled baking sheet and cook for 15 minutes or until golden. Try rolling in seeds, chopped dried fruit, or parmesan cheese before cooking. Yield: 36 bread sticks.

193

Apple Potato Folds

Ingredients

1/2 cup unbleached flour
5 or 6 potatoes
2 sliced, peeled apples
1/2 teaspoon salt
4 tablespoons butter
Cinnamon and sugar

Directions

Boil the potatoes and mash well, making sure there are no lumps.
Mix in the flour and knead to make a pliable dough. Roll dough into
a circle. Put the apple slices on one half of the dough. Sprinkle
apples with cinnamon and sugar, dab butter on top. Fold other half
of dough over apples and pinch around edges to seal. Cook over
medium heat in a frying pan until apples are cooked and dough is
golden. Serve in slices. Yield: 12 to 18 servings.

194

Oven-Fried Chicken

Ingredients

2 1/2 pounds (1kg) chicken cut up
1/4 cup unbleached flour
2 eggs
1 1/2 teaspoons salt
1 tablespoon paprika
1/2 teaspoon onion salt
1 tablespoon lemon juice
1 tablespoon honey
1/4 cup margarine
1 cup Italian seasoned bread crumbs

Directions

Preheat oven to 350°F (180°C). Shake the chicken pieces in a bag with the flour. Beat together the eggs, salt, paprika, onion salt, lemon juice, and honey. Melt the margarine in a small saucepan. Dip the floured chicken, one piece at a time, in the egg mixture, then in the crumbs, turning to coat evenly, and then in the butter. Arrange the chicken, skin side down in a 9x13 inch baking dish. Bake for 45 minutes, or until fork tender. Turn once during baking. Serve at once or cool and pack for a picnic. Yield 6 to 8 servings.

195

R.G. Gorp

Ingredients

2 cups chocolate or carob chips
2 cups raisins
2 cups peanuts

Directions

Place ingredients in a large bowl and stir until mixed. Put in airtight container or bags and bring on an outing!

196

Activity: As you eat your picnic, lie on your backs and look at the clouds. Imagine what they could be.

Crepe Sandwich Rolls

Ingredients
1 cup unbleached flour
1/2 teaspoon salt
2 eggs
1 cup milk
Oil for cooking
10 thin slices ham or turkey
1/4 cup light cream cheese
2 tomatoes sliced paper thin

Directions
Put the flour and 1/2 teaspoon salt in a small bowl and add the eggs. Beat until well mixed, then gradually add milk, beating constantly to make a smooth batter. Brush a small non-stick shallow pan with oil and place over medium heat. Pour in 1 tablespoon batter at a time and swirl it around to make a very thin pancake. Cook for about 1 minute, until pale brown, then turn. repeat until you have 6 pancakes. Lay a pancake on the counter and put a slice of meat on it. Add another pancake, then a layer of cream cheese. Another pancake, then a layer of tomato. Continue repeating until 6 pancakes are on pile. Roll into a cylinder and chill for 1 hour. When ready to eat cut in thin slices. Yield: 6 servings.

197

Parties

Seems like only yesterday
that he was turning three
bean bag toss and relay races
played around the tree.

Ice cream cones and red balloons
on decorated mats,
funny clowns and magic tricks
pointed birthday hats.

Now I notice posters,
tapes of rock and roll
hot dogs, punch and pretzels,
popcorn in a bowl.

Books on monster movies
skates of black and gray
a cake with baseball figures
he's turning ten today.

Time Saving Truffle

Ingredients
1 pound cake
2 small packages instant vanilla pudding
4 cups fresh fruit
Natural jam

Directions
Cut pound cake in half lengthwise. Spread jam in-between cake.
Cut cake into cubes. Set aside. Make the instant pudding. Prepare
fruit, cut into small pieces. Layer in a glass dish, starting with 1/2 of
the cake cubes, 1/2 the pudding, followed by 1/2 the fruit. Repeat
ending with fruit on top. Refrigerate until serving. Top with whipped
topping if desired. Yield: 8 to 10 servings

198

Question: Describe the best birthday party you could imagine.

Egg Cups

Ingredients
1   loaf whole-grain sandwich bread, sliced
1/4 cup margarine
2/3 cup cheese, grated
4   hard-boiled eggs
1   small can cheddar cheese soup, undiluted
1   teaspoon dry mustard
Salt and pepper

Directions
Preheat oven to 350°F (180°C). Remove crusts from slices of bread. Brush slices with melted butter and press quickly and firmly into deep muffin pans. Bake for 15-20 minutes or until crisp. In a saucepan, heat and mix soup with grated cheese, mustard, salt, pepper, and chopped hard-boiled eggs. Fill warm egg mixture into warm breadcases and serve immediately. Try using other creative combinations in the bread cups or let children assemble their dinner at the table! Yield: 18 egg cups.

199

Ham/Turkey Roll Ups

Ingredients
8 ounces (225g) light cream cheese
1 tablespoon milk
1 pound of sliced boiled ham or turkey

Directions
Beat the cream cheese with milk until light and fluffy. Spread onto the slices of ham or turkey. Roll up like a jelly-roll, starting at the narrow end. Wrap in foil and chill. When ready to serve suggest that your child make a design out of the roll-ups; try stars, flowers, trees or hearts. See how many different shapes can be made. Yield: 10 to 12 rolls.

200

Vegetable Dip

Ingredients
1/2 cup natural peanut butter
1/2 cup plain lowfat yogurt
2 tablespoon maple syrup
Raw carrot curls
Pretzel sticks
Celery stalks
Pieces of fruit
Bread sticks

Directions
Blend the peanut butter (at room temperature), yogurt, and maple syrup together. Wash, peel, cut, and prepare dipping foods. Set on the table and see the excitement this dip and serve treat will add to any child's gathering!

201

Ice Cream Cone Cakes

Ingredients
Flat bottomed ice-cream cones
Cake mix
Frosting mix
Cake decorations
Muffin pan

Directions
Prepare cake mix according to directions. Spoon the
batter into the cones until they are 2/3 full. Place the
cones in the muffin pan and bake at 350°F (180°C)
for 12 to 15 minutes. When cool, frost and decorate.
Yield: 12 to 15 cupcakes.

Activity: *Tell your child something about the day
they were born.*

202

Claw Bread Sticks

Ingredients

11-ounce (315g) can refrigerated soft
   breadsticks
2 tablespoons margarine, melted
8 thin slices ham, turkey, or chicken; cut
   diagonally in half
8 thin slices cheese cut diagonally in half
16 thin apple slices

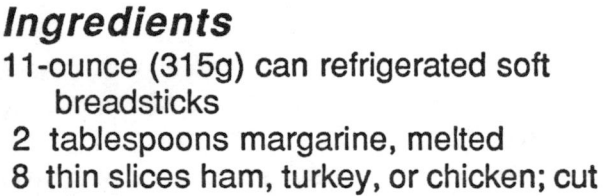

Directions

Preheat oven to 350°F (180C). Unroll
dough; separate into 8 strips. Cut strips in
half to form 16 smaller strips. Place one
inch apart on ungreased cookie sheet.
Using a knife, cut the end of each stick to
form a claw shape. Bake for 11 to 15
minutes. Remove from cookie sheet and
cool. Wrap one ham triangle and one
cheese triangle around stick halfway up;
top with apple slice. Yield: 16 bread sticks.

Mealtime Question: *Getting along with others is hard to learn.
Ask your child who he or she dislikes the most. Then ask what is
the best thing about that person.*

203

Small Stack Sandwich

Ingredients
1/4 cup margarine
1/8 teaspoon salt
1 tablespoon lemon juice
3 ounces (85g) cream cheese or kefir cheese
5 thin slices of natural white bread
10 thin slices whole grain bread
20 thin tomato slices
20 thin cucumber slices

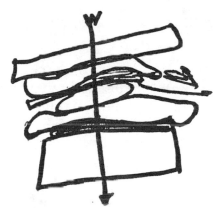

Directions
Mix together margarine, lemon juice, salt, and cream cheese.
Using a round cookie cutter, cut 20 circles from the white bread,
and 40 circles from the whole wheat bread. Using the same cutter
cut one circle from each tomato and cucumber slice. Spread 1/2
teaspoon cheese mixture on one side of each bread. To
assemble layer grain circle, tomato, white circle, cucumber, and
grain circle. Put a toothpick through the sandwich and serve.
Yield: 6 to 8 servings.

204

Go Fish

Ingredients

13 ounces (375g) tuna drained and flaked
1 medium potato, peeled and quartered
1/4 cup tartar sauce
1 tablespoon parsley
1 teaspoon lemon juice
Salt and pepper to taste
1 egg, beaten
1 tablespoon water
24 finely crushed cracker crumbs

Directions

Preheat oven to 375°F (190°C). In a small saucepan boil potato in salted water for 15 minutes. Drain and mash. Stir in tuna, tartar sauce, parsley, and lemon juice. Season. Divide the tuna mixture into 8 portions. Shape each portion into a fish (about 3/4" thick). Place the cracker crumbs on a plate. Dip the fish into the egg then into the crumbs. Place fish on a greased baking sheet. Bake for 15 to 20 minutes. Serve with tartar sauce or ketchup.
Yield: 8 servings.

205

Note: *Play a game—have the kids make up stories about fish!*

A Cool Cake

Ingredients

Favorite cake mix
Vanilla icing
Vegetable food coloring
Corn syrup
Chocolate syrup
5 paper cups

Directions

Bake cake according to package directions. Spread the icing over the cake as smoothly as possible. Pour 2 tablespoons of corn syrup into each of 4 paper cups. Next add a different food color to each cup and add chocolate syrup to the fifth cup. Drip the colors onto the cake using spoons. Let the colors run together or mix them up and experiment with patterning. Yield: 8 servings.

Note: *For an interesting birthday cake, wait until the guests are seated and pass the iced cake around for everyone to decorate!*

206

Tiny Piney Burgers

Ingredients

8 ounces of soft tofu
1 pound lean ground beef or turkey
1 cup chopped, drained pineapple
2 tablespoons mustard
1 tablespoon honey
Whole grain crackers or bread

Directions

In a large bowl, mash the tofu. Add the ground beef or turkey and mix well. Roll into meatballs and flatten. Add 1 tablespoon oil to skillet and cook burgers over medium heat until done. While burgers are cooking, blend the pineapple, mustard, and honey until smooth. Drain the burgers and place on crackers or bread (cut with cookie cutters into circles). Yield: 8 to 10 servings.

207

Party Rice

Ingredients

2 1/3 cups long grain white rice
3/4 cup butter or margarine
1/2 cup grated parmesan cheese
2 eggs
1/4 cup grated Swiss cheese
5 slices smoked cooked ham
5 slices mozzarella cheese
1/4 teaspoon grated nutmeg
1 teaspoon chopped basil
Salt and pepper to taste

Directions

Boil the rice in salted water until tender. Drain well, place in a bowl and mix with 6 tablespoons butter, nutmeg, and parmesan cheese. Preheat oven to 350°F (180°C). Beat the eggs in a bowl with the Swiss cheese, salt, pepper, basil, and garlic. Mix well. Melt 2 tablespoons butter into an omelette pan and pour in the egg mixture. Allow to cook until firm, turning over once. Butter a round 10 inch mold. Line the bottom with rice, arrange half the ham on top and place omelette over this, followed by slices of mozzarella and remaining ham. Cover with rice. Dot with butter and bake 15 minutes. Serve hot.
Yield: 6 servings.

208

Fruitin' Tootin' Dip

Ingredients
6 ounces (170g) cream cheese or kefir cheese
1/4 cup powdered sugar
1/4 cup frozen limeade, thawed
2 cups natural lowfat vanilla yogurt
Assorted fruit cut and peeled

Directions
In a small bowl, combine cheese, powdered sugar, and limeade; beat until well blended. Add yogurt and blend until smooth. Put bowl in center of large plate. Let child arrange fruit in their own design, then dig in. Kids love to dip and eat! Yield: Varies according to fruit used.

Note: *If parents would approach eating as a natural and social event, they would teach good eating habits to their children. Nagging and scolding only serve to reinforce poor eating habits.*

209

Raspberry Clouds

Ingredients
3 egg whites
1 cup powdered sugar
1 1/4 cups whipping cream
4 cups fresh raspberries

Directions
Preheat oven to 325°F (170°C). Put the egg whites in a mixing bowl and beat until stiff. Fold in the powdered sugar, then beat again until smooth, satiny, and standing in peaks. Line two baking trays with wax paper. Spoon egg whites onto trays making 3-inch round circles. Bake until dry and light but not golden (3 to 5 minutes). Meanwhile whip the cream and sweeten it with 2 tablespoons sugar. Add a few of the raspberries, folding gently so they don't get squashed. Place one meringue on bottom, cream in-between, top with other meringue. Chill for 1 hour. Puree the remaining raspberries, and serve separately as a sauce.
Yield: 8 to 10 servings.

210

Hot Dogs in Sleeping Bags

Ingredients

1 loaf frozen bread dough, thawed
10 turkey, chicken, or tofu hot dogs
Ketchup, mustard, and pickle relish
1 pressurized can cheddar-cheese spread
Chopped green pepper
Corn snack horns

Directions

Divide the dough into 10 pieces. On a floured surface roll each piece into a 10x2 inch rectangle. Place hot dog lengthwise on end of each rectangle. Spread mustard, ketchup and relish on other half of dough. Fold dough to cover all but 1/4 of the hot dog. Pinch edges closed with fingers. Place on greased baking sheet. Cover and let rise for 30 minutes. Preheat oven to 375°F (190°C). Bake for 15 minutes or until brown. Cool slightly and decorate with cheese for hair, green peppers for eyes, and horns for hats. Night, night! Yield: 8 to 10 servings.

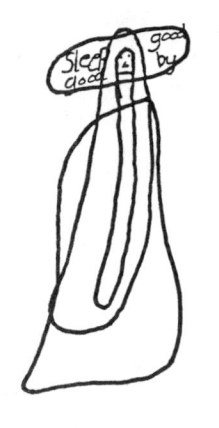

211

Turkish Jello Candy

Ingredients

4 packages of unflavored gelatin
1 cup cold water
3 small packages of jello
1/2 cup sugar
4 cups boiling water
Powdered sugar

Directions

Have ready a glass 9x13x2 inch pan. In a large pitcher, mix together the gelatin and cold water. Let it sit for 5 minutes. Add the jello and sugar then pour in the boiling water. Stir until the mixture is clear and all the crystals are dissolved. Pour the mixture into the pan and then let set in the refrigerator overnight. Using a wet knife, cut into one inch cubes. Roll each cube in the powdered sugar until well-coated and serve as a finger food dessert or candy. Yield: Varies.

212

Ice-Cream Snow Balls

Ingredients
3 cups flaked coconut
1/2 gallon natural vanilla ice cream

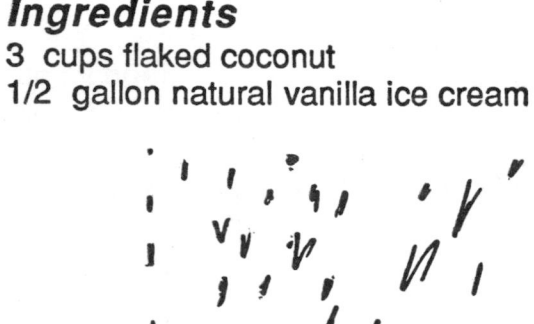

Directions
Line a large cookie sheet with waxed paper.
Make ice cream into 16 separate balls. Place
on cookie sheet and freeze until firm. Put
coconut on a plate and remove ice cream
balls from freezer. Quickly, roll each ball in
coconut and return to freeze until firm.
Yield: 6 to 8 snow balls.

Note: *Children's appetites vary from day to
day. Vary your menus while at the same time
keep them nutritious and appealing.*

213

Tea Party Snacks

Ingredients
3 hard-boiled eggs
2/3 cup crushed pineapple
1/2 cup cottage cheese
salt and pepper
savory crackers
butter for spreading

Directions
Chop hard-boiled eggs and mix with pineapple, cottage cheese, salt, and pepper. Spread crisp, savory crackers with butter and top with egg and pineapple spread. Serve with beverage in small tea cups.

214

Pasta

Oregano and Garlic
Sauce by the Oodles
Tomato and Basil
Fresh Pasta Noodles

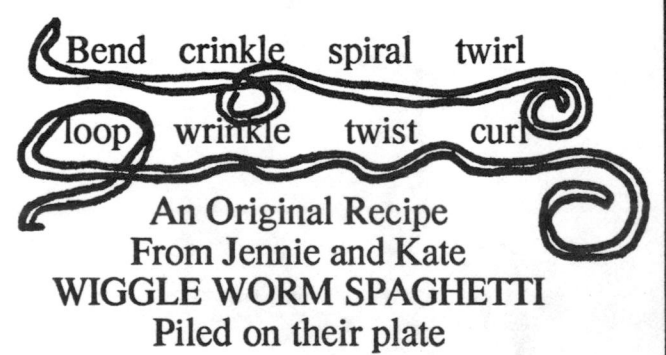

Bend crinkle spiral twirl
loop wrinkle twist curl

An Original Recipe
From Jennie and Kate
WIGGLE WORM SPAGHETTI
Piled on their plate

Macaroni And Cheese

Ingredients

1/2 pound (450g) macaroni
2 tablespoons margarine
2 tablespoons flour
2 cups milk
1 teaspoon salt
1 teaspoon mustard
1 cup grated cheddar cheese
1 egg

Directions

Preheat oven to 400°F (200°C). Put 4 quarts cold water in a large pot and boil. Sprinkle macaroni into boiling water and cook 10 minutes. To make the sauce; melt margarine over medium heat, stir in flour with a whisk. Add milk and cook, stirring constantly with the whisk, until it is slightly thickened with no lumps. Remove from heat, stir in 1 teaspoon salt, pepper, mustard, and cheese. Drain the macaroni and place in a greased casserole dish. Pour sauce over and bake for 20 minutes. Yield: 6 servings.

215

Homemade Noodles

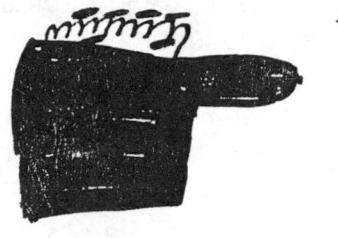

Ingredients
2 cups unbleached flour
5 eggs
1 tablespoon olive oil

Directions
Sift the flour in a pile onto a work surface. Make a well in the center of the flour. Break the eggs into the center, add the oil, mix with a fork, and work the dough with hands until smooth and elastic. Roll out with a rolling pin, or use a pasta maker, until very thin. Leave the pasta to dry, sprinkle with flour, then roll up the sheet of pasta gently. With a knife, cut into thin strips. Sprinkle with flour. Cook in boiling water until pasta floats to the top and is tender. Serve with butter, sauces, herbs, and spices. Be creative!
Yield: 4 servings.

Activity: Save all the empty cartons you cooked with today and let your child build something out of them, as you make dinner.

216

Big Meatball Stew

Ingredients

1/2 pound (250g) ground beef
1/2 pound (250g) ground turkey
2 slices bread, crumbled
1/2 cup milk
1 egg, beaten
1 cup tomato sauce
1 large onion, chopped

Salt and pepper to taste
2 tablespoons vegetable oil
2 carrots, peeled and diced
2 cups beef broth or bouillon
2 tablespoons tomato paste
1 package frozen peas
1 pound (500g) spaghetti

Directions

In a large bowl, combine the beef, turkey, bread, milk, egg, 1/4 cup tomato sauce, 1/4 onion, salt, and pepper. Stir until blended. Set aside. In a large saucepan, heat oil and add remaining onion and carrots. Saute. Add broth, remaining tomato sauce and tomato paste. Bring to a boil. Let simmer while forming meatballs. Wet hands and shape meat mixture into 6 - 8 meatballs about 2 1/2 inches across. Drop meatballs into hot stock and simmer for 30 minutes, covered. Add peas and cook another 5 minutes. Cook spaghetti according to directions. Toss with 2 tablespoons butter and 1 tablespoon grated Parmesan cheese. Serve one meatball per person over cooked spaghetti with sauce.

217

Crunch A Lunch Spaghetti

Ingredients

1 cup thin spaghetti, broken into 2-3"
   pieces
1 can tomato soup
1 cup water
1 fresh tomato, peeled and diced
1/2 teaspoon Italian seasoning

Directions

Combine soup, water, tomato, and seasoning in a medium-size saucepan. Bring to a boil and stir in spaghetti so that all pieces are covered by liquid. Cover tightly, remove from heat, and let stand 30 minutes. Serve warm or cold. Yield: 4 servings.

Note: *Dorothy Corkille Briggs, author of Your Child's Self Esteem (New York: Doubleday, 1975) writes that various factors combine to make you the parent a most crucial mirror in your child's life... your reflections of your child are the first your child experiences. This is because your child is dependent upon you for physical, social, and emotional satisfactions. (p. 15)*

218

Flowering Spinach Lasagne

Ingredients

Favorite jar of spaghetti sauce
1 large bunch spinach; or 1 10-ounce package
   frozen chopped spinach (thawed)
1 pound ricotta cheese
1 cup shredded lowfat mozzarella cheese

1 egg
1/4 teaspoon pepper
1/4 teaspoon ground nutmeg
8 lasagne noodles
Boiling, salted water
Parsley

Directions

Pick tough stems from spinach. Rinse leaves well; place leaves just covered with water in a 4-quart pan. Cook over medium heat, stirring often, just until wilted (about 3 minutes) cool, press out water and chop. Stir together spinach, cheeses, egg, pepper, and nutmeg. Cook lasagne according to package directions. Pour spaghetti sauce into a greased shallow casserole. To assemble flowers; pat noodle dry, cut in half lengthwise. Spread about 1/4 cup cheese mixture over noodle and roll up like a jelly roll. Stand flowers, curly edges up, in the casserole on top of the sauce. Cover and bake in a 350°F (180°C) oven until heated through (about 30 minutes).

219

Chicken Fruit Pasta Salad

Ingredients

8 ounces (225g) pineapple chunks
4 halved chicken breasts, cooked and
   cut into bite-size pieces
1 stalk celery, chopped
1 cup seedless grapes
8 ounces (225g) rotelle (pasta shaped like twists)

Pineapple Mayonnaise

1 cup light mayonnaise
2 tablespoons pineapple juice, drained from can
1 teaspoon fresh lemon juice

Directions

Drain pineapple chunks and reserve juice for dressing. Prepare pineapple mayonnaise. Place chicken, celery, grapes, and pineapple in a large bowl, refrigerate until ready to use. Cook pasta according to package directions. Add pasta to chicken bowl. Add pineapple mayonnaise, salt, and pepper. Yield: 4 servings.

220

Broccoli Mushroom Lasagne

Ingredients

8 ounces (250g) lasagne noodles, cooked
1 packet (250g) chopped brocoli, cooked
2 cups low fat cottage cheese
1 can mushroom soup

8 ounces (250g) mozzarella cheese, grated
1/2 cup parmesan cheese, grated
Ground pepper to taste
10 - 12 fresh mushrooms, sliced

Directions

Preheat oven to 350°F (180°C). Lightly cook fresh mushrooms and ground pepper in a small saucepan with 2 tablespoons water. Combine with mushroom soup and spread mixture on the bottom of a 9 x 13 inch pan. Layer 1/3 of the noodles on top then layer 1/3 broccoli, 1/3 cottage cheese, and 1/3 of the cheeses. Continue to layer ingredients with the cheeses being the last. Add extra mozzarella cheese on top if desired. Bake for 45 minutes. Let stand for 20 minutes before cutting into squares. Serve with a green salad and bread. Yield: 8 servings.

Note: When you have dinner all ready and almost everything on the table, play this little before dinner game. Ask your child what is missing on the table. It could be someone's fork or napkin or glass. Reverse roles and let your child remove something and you guess what's missing.

221

Mac and Cheese Omelet

Ingredients

1-2 tablespoons butter or margarine
4 eggs, lightly beaten
1 cup leftover cooked macaroni and cheese
1/2 teaspoon salt
2 tablespoons grated romano cheese

Directions

In a medium-size frying pan, heat butter over medium heat. Combine remaining ingredients until well blended. When margarine is melted, pour in egg mixture and cook just until bottom and sides are set. Remove from heat. Loosen omelet with a spatula; flip over on one side folding the omelet in half; cover pan and let stand for a few minutes until the center is set. Yield: 4 servings.

222

Activity: As you cook and eat, communicate only through songs.

Donna's Noodle Rice

Ingredients

1/2 cup butter
5 fideo noodles, crunched
2 cans full strength chicken broth
1 cup rice (not instant)
1/4 cup water
1/4 cup sherry wine

Directions

Melt butter in a large frying pan. Lightly brown fideo
noodles. Add broth and rice, bring to a boil. Add
water and sherry. Cover and cook over low heat for
approximately 30 minutes or until rice is soft.
Yield: 6 servings.

*Activity: Have your child make a centerpiece for
the dinner table. (Fill a shallow bowl with sand and
stick things in it.)*

223

Gnochi

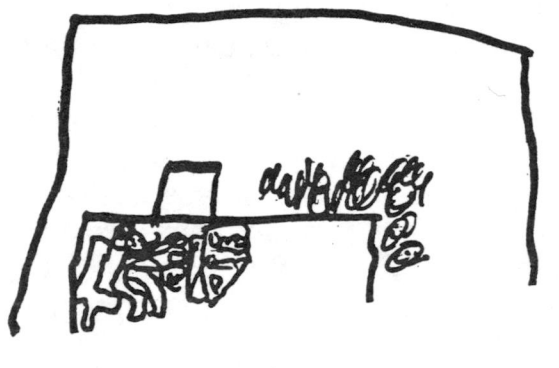

Ingredients

5 tablespoons butter
1/2 cup unbleached flour
2 1/4 cups chicken broth
2 eggs
1/2 cup grated parmesan cheese
1/4 teaspoon nutmeg
3/4 cup tomato sauce
3 tablespoons cream
1 teaspoon basil

Directions

Melt the butter in a small pan and stir in the flour. Add the broth and stir vigorously. Cook, stirring constantly, until the mixture draws away from the sides of the pan. Remove from heat. Stir in the eggs, (one at a time) cheese, and nutmeg. Heat water to boiling in a large pan and drop the dough into the water by the teaspoon. Cook for 10 minutes. Strain. Add tomato sauce, cream and basil. Cook until warmed and serve. Yield: 4 servings.

224

Lazy Lasagne

Ingredients

2 cans stewed tomatoes
1 small can tomato paste
Italian spices or herbs
2 eggs
2 cups ricotta cheese

1 pound (500g) ground beef
1 package lasagne noodles
1 cup mozzarella cheese
1/4 cup parmesan cheese

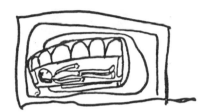

Directions

First prepare the sauce. Mix the cans of tomatoes with the tomato paste and season with Italian spices and herbs. Stir until well blended. Lightly beat the eggs in a large bowl and blend in the ricotta cheese. Brown the ground beef in a skillet (or cook in the microwave). Drain off excess fat. Add the meat to the tomato sauce mixture. Spread 1/3 of the sauce on the bottom of a lasagne pan. Cover with a layer of dry noodles and then spread with 1/2 of the egg and cheese mixture. Repeat layering this way until the ingredients are used up and a layer of meat sauce is on the top. Cover with a plastic wrap and microwave on high for 12 minutes. Remove wrap and sprinkle with mozzarella and Parmesan cheeses. Bake uncovered in a conventional oven for another 20 - 30 minutes. Cool before serving. Yield: 6 - 8 servings.

225

White Rice

Ingredients

2 cups water
1/2 teaspoon salt
1 tablespoon butter
1 cup long grain white rice

Optional additions

Beans, nuts, vegetables,
eggs, seasoning, juices, etc.

Directions

Place water in saucepan; add salt and butter. Bring to a boil. Stir in the rice. Reduce heat to low, cover tightly, and simmer without removing cover for 20 to 25 minutes. If you would like to, add optional juices to water when boiling, or add additions when rice is finished. Yield: 4 servings.

226

Bacon And Eggs Spaghetti

Ingredients

1/4 cup real bacon bits
1 pound (450 g) spaghetti
1/2 cup butter
1 peeled clove of garlic
1/3 cup fresh parsley
1/2 cup grated parmesan cheese
2 eggs
2 hard-boiled eggs chopped

Directions

In a large pot bring 4 quarts of water to a boil. Add spaghetti and cook for 10 minutes. While spaghetti is cooking, prepare the sauce. Put butter and garlic in a small pan. Melt over low heat, add 2 eggs and beat for a minute or so. When the spaghetti is done strain in a colander. Put it in a large bowl. Take the garlic out of the egg mixture, pour over the spaghetti and mix it up quickly. Sprinkle cheese, hard-boiled eggs, and bacon bits on top, mix together and serve warm. Yield: 8 servings.

227

Apple Risotto

Ingredients

4 apples
Juice from 1/2 lemon
5 tablespoons butter
1/3 cup olive oil
1 2/3 cups risotto rice
1/4 cup dry white wine
1 quart (1 litre) beef or chicken broth
1/2 cup grated parmesan cheese
Dash of nutmeg, salt, and pepper

Directions

Peel the apples, remove the core and cut into cubes. Bring a pan of water and lemon juice to a boil. Immerse the apples, bring back to a boil and cook for 3 minutes. Drain and place in a small pan with 1 tablespoon of the butter, fry until golden brown. Remove and keep warm. Place pan over medium heat. Put 2 tablespoons butter in a pan with oil. Sprinkle in the rice and let it turn golden. Add the wine and broth. Stir from time to time to mix well. Add the apples after 10 minutes and continue to stir. Just before the rice is cooked add the cheese, salt, pepper, nutmeg and remaining butter. Serve warm. Yield: 6 servings.

228

Mac Roni's Cold Salad

Ingredients

16 ounces (450g) uncooked spiral macaroni
1 1/2 cups diced dill pickles
1 1/2 cups shredded carrots
16 ounces (450g) sweet peas, thawed
6 ounces pineapple tid bits (optional)

Dressing

1 3/4 cups natural mayonnaise
1 cup natural plain yogurt
1/3 cup dill pickle juice
2 tablespoons honey
1/2 teaspoon dry mustard
Salt and pepper to taste

Directions

Cook macaroni according to package. Drain and rinse with cold water. In a large bowl, combine the salad ingredients and blend well. In small bowl combine the dressing ingredients. Pour dressing over salad and stir to coat. Yield: 8 to 12 servings.

229

Rice Mold

Ingredients

1 tablespoon chopped parsley
1 teaspoon chopped basil
1 clove garlic
1 onion, sliced
1/2 cup white wine
1 2/3 cups risotto rice
1 quart (1 lliter) chicken broth
1/4 cup grated parmesan cheese
2 tomatoes, sliced and peeled
7 thick slices mozzarella cheese

Directions

Preheat oven to 400°F (200°C). Finely chop the herbs and garlic together. Place the onion in a large pan with the wine, cook for 4 minutes. Sprinkle in the rice, add the broth and simmer until the rice is al dente (about 15 minutes). Add the herbs, garlic, and cheese. Pour half the rice into a non-stick cake pan or ring mold, season with salt and pepper. Cover with slices of peeled tomato and mozzarella cheese. Cover with remaining risotto. Bake for 20 minutes. Turn out on to a warm serving dish. Yield: 4 servings.

230

Macaroni Cheese Medley

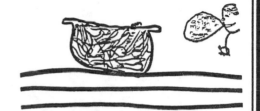

Ingredients
1 14-ounce (400g) packet macaroni and cheese dinner
1 10-ounce (275g) package frozen spinach
1 cup sour cream or plain yogurt
6 crisply cooked bacon slices

Directions
Prepare the macaroni and cheese dinner as directed on package.
Thaw the spinach and drain. Squeeze out as much moisture as
possible. Add the spinach, sour cream, and crumbled bacon to the
macaroni and cheese dinner. Mix well. Heat thoroughly, stirring
often, but do not let boil. Yield 4 - 6 servings.

Note: *Peas or another green vegetable can be substituted for
spinach. Also, a 6 1/2 ounce (175g) can of tuna, drained and
flaked, can be substituted for bacon.*

231

Peanut Butter

Peanut Butter Brownies
Peanut Butter Soup
Peanut Butter Milkshakes
The Favorite of my Group.

Munchy...Crunchy...
Sticky...Chewey...
Hunky...Chunky...
Creamy...Gooey...

Nutritiously delicious
Each and every bite
Hooray for Peanut Butter
Morning, Noon or Night!

Peanutty Pancakes

Ingredients

1 cup natural chunky peanut butter
1/2 cup margarine, melted
2 eggs
1 1/2 cups unbleached flour
1 teaspoon sugar
1 1/2 teaspoons baking powder
Pinch of salt
1 1/2 cups milk

Directions

In a large bowl, beat together the peanut butter and margarine until smooth. Beat in the eggs, one at a time. In another bowl, sift the dry ingredients together. Add the flour mixture to the egg mixture alternately with the milk. Stir until thoroughly combined and let the batter stand 1 hour covered with a cloth. Heat a skillet to medium heat and grease lightly. Using a 1/4 cup measure, drop the batter onto the skillet to form 3" round pancakes. Brown on both sides and dig in! Yield: 4 servings.

232

Note: Dr. George Washington Carver spent 50 years studying the peanut plant. He discovered over 300 uses for peanuts; including soap, ink, dye, floor coverings, cosmetic cream and peanut butter.

Peanut Apple Cookies

Ingredients

1/2 cup margarine, softened
1/2 cup natural peanut butter
2 eggs
2 teaspoons vanilla
1/4 cup apple juice concentrate, thawed
1/4 cup brown sugar
1 1/2 cups unbleached flour
1/2 teaspoon baking soda

Directions

Preheat oven to 375°F (190°C). Cream margarine until fluffy. Blend in peanut butter, eggs, vanilla, apple juice, and brown sugar; beat until creamy. Stir in dry ingredients until well mixed. Drop by tablespoons onto a greased baking sheet. Flatten the cookie with a fork (a good job for little hands). Bake 10 minutes or until done. Cool. Yield: 24 cookies.

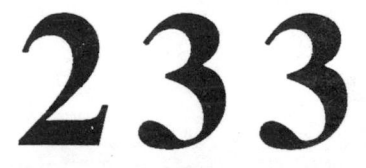

233

Peanut Butter Oatmeal!

Ingredients

4 cups lowfat milk
2 cups rolled oats (not instant)
4 teaspoons peanut butter
4 teaspoons honey

Directions

Heat milk to almost boiling, slowly add oats stirring constantly. Reduce heat and cook about 10 minutes or until thickened. Pour into bowls and add one teaspoon peanut butter and one teaspoon honey to each. Stir well. Yield: 4 servings.

234

Chicken Dunkers

Ingredients

4 boneless, skinless, chicken breasts
1/4 cup natural peanut butter
4 tablespoons honey
Butter or oil for frying

Directions

Cut chicken breasts into thin strips. Put in frying pan over medium heat with oil or butter. Fry until tender and brown. Drain on paper towels. Mix peanut butter with honey and pour into a bowl. Put bowl in the center of the plate. Place chicken strips around the bowl and serve. Dunk chicken in peanut butter honey sauce.
Yield: 4 servings.

235

P. B. and Pineapple Sandwiches

Ingredients

2/3 cup natural chunk-style peanut butter
1 1/2 ounces (40g) package cream cheese, softened
1/2 cup drained crushed pineapple
1/4 cup shredded carrot
8 slices whole-grain sandwich bread

Directions

In a small bowl stir together the peanut butter and softened cream cheese.
Stir in the pineapple and carrot. Spread the mixture on 4 slices of the bread
and top with the remaining slices. Yield: 4 servings.

Note: *Given enough time and freedom of choice, children will
develop a taste for many foods ... but children, especially younger
ones, are traditionalists. They are reluctant to try new things. From
The Practical Parent by Genevieve Painter and Raymond Corsini,
(New York: Simon & Schuster, 1984), p. 56.*

236

Pete's Pudding

Ingredients
1   ripe banana
1/2 cup natural nonfat yogurt
1/2 cup natural peanut butter
1/4 teaspoon vanilla
Banana to slice

Directions
Combine all ingredients except banana in a blender or food
processor. Process on low then high until smooth. Pour into four
dishes and refrigerate for 1 to 2 hours. Cut banana slices over top
before serving. Yield: 4 servings.

237

Mr. P.B. Blueberry Muffins

Ingredients

1/2 cup natural peanut butter
2 eggs
4 tablespoons honey
3/4 cup lowfat milk
2 cups whole-wheat pastry flour
2 teaspoons baking powder
1/2 cup fresh or frozen blueberries
1 jar natural blueberry jam

Directions

Preheat oven to 375ºF (190ºC). Place paper or foil muffin cups in muffin tin. Combine peanut butter, eggs, honey, and milk. Mix well. Put blueberries in bowl, cover with flour and baking powder. Fold the blueberry and flour mixture into the peanut butter mixture. Fill tins 3/4 full with batter. Put a teaspoon of jam on top and swirl through batter with a toothpick (Don't give to child under three). Bake 20 minutes. Yield: 12 to 18 muffins.

238

Peanut Popcorn

Ingredients

1 cup sugar
3/4 cup margarine
1/3 cup water
1/4 cup natural peanut butter
1 tablespoon light corn syrup
8 cups popped popcorn
1 cup peanuts

Directions

Warning: this recipe is not for children under three years.
Combine sugar, margarine, water, peanut butter, and corn syrup in a saucepan over medium heat. Stir constantly until boiling. Continue cooking until candy thermometer reads 240°F (120°C) (soft ball stage). Remove unpopped kernels from popped corn. Combine popcorn and peanuts in a greased 13x9-inch pan. Pour syrup mixture over popcorn and stir gently to coat popcorn. Bake in a 300°F (150°C) oven for 5 minutes. Pour onto foil and cool completely. Store in an airtight container or break into clusters and eat! Yield: 8 servings.

239

Edible Play Dough

Ingredients
1 cup natural peanut butter
3 tablespoons honey
1/2 cup powdered milk
Cocoa or carob powder
Powdered milk
Raisins and other edibles

Directions
Place peanut butter, honey, and powdered milk into a bowl. Mix
with fingers. Add more powdered milk if play dough is too sticky.
Add cocoa or carob if so desired. Make shapes and add other
foods for eyes, hair ect. Eat when finished.

240

Peanut Butter and Chocolate Drink

Ingredients

Hot chocolate (mix or homemade)
1 teaspoon creamy peanut butter
Whipped cream (optional)
Chocolate-covered peanut butter candies (optional)

Directions

Prepare cup(s) of hot chocolate. Dissolve peanut butter in hot chocolate. Garnish with whipped cream and top with chocolate-covered peanut butter candies. Serve with cookies or fruit. Yield: 1 cup per person.

Note: *My father made us cups of hot chocolate on winter nights before we went to bed. Here is his recipe:* **Homemade Hot Chocolate**: *Put 1teaspoon cocoa, 1 teaspoon sugar, and 1 tablespoon of milk in a cup and stir until very smooth and shiny. Slowly add scalded milk while continuing to stir. Add a drop of vanilla and sprinkle cinnamon or nutmeg on top.*

241

P.B. Chip Muffins

Ingredients

1 1/2 cups unbleached flour
1/3 cup sugar or 1/4 cup maple syrup
2 1/2 teaspoons baking powder
1/4 teaspoon salt
1/2 cup natural chunk-style peanut butter
2 tablespoons butter or margarine
2 beaten eggs
3/4 cup milk
1/2 cup chocolate or carob pieces

Directions

Preheat oven to 400°F (200°C). In a medium bowl stir together the flour, sugar, baking powder, and salt. With a pastry blender or 2 knives cut in the chunk-style peanut butter and the butter until the mixture resembles coarse crumbs. In a small bowl combine the eggs and milk. Add all at once to the flour mixture. Stir just till moistened; Batter should be lumpy. Fold in chocolate pieces. Fill muffin cups 2/3 full and bake 15 to 17 minutes. Yield: 12 servings.

242

Peanut Butter Granola

Ingredients

3 cups rolled oats
1 cup coconut
1 cup unsalted peanuts
1/2 cup sunflower seeds
1/2 cup toasted wheat germ
2/3 cup natural peanut butter
1/2 cup light corn syrup
1/4 cup packed brown sugar
2 tablespoons cooking oil
1/2 cup raisins

Directions

Preheat oven to 300°F (150°C). Stir together the oats, coconut, peanuts, sunflower seeds, and toasted wheat germ. Set aside. In a small saucepan combine the peanut butter, corn syrup, brown sugar, and cooking oil. Cook and stir over medium heat until the peanut butter is melted and the brown sugar is dissolved. Pour the peanut butter mixture over the oat mixture. Stir until mixed. Spread mixture in a 15x10x1 inch baking pan. Bake 45 minutes. Stir every 15 minutes to prevent burning. Once the mixture is out of the oven stir in the raisins. Cool completely before placing in a container. Yield: 16 half cup servings.

243

Note: *Peanuts, seeds, and nuts are for children over three years.*

Peanut Butter Biscuits

Ingredients

1/3 cup margarine
1/2 cup natural peanut butter
1/4 cup brown sugar
3/4 cup whole-grain flour
1 large egg
3/4 teaspoon baking soda
Raw or plain sugar

Directions

Preheat oven to 350°F (180°C). Place all ingredients except raw sugar in bowl and mix to form stiff dough. Shape dough with hands into small balls (get the small hands to help you!). Put raw sugar on a small plate. Put peanut ball on the plate and flatten slightly into the sugar. Place sugar side up on the cookie sheet. Bake for 15 to 20 minutes. Cool and eat! Yield: 12 to 18 cookies.

244

No Bake Apricot Drops

Ingredients
1 1/2 cups natural peanut butter
1 cup dried apricots
1/4 cup honey
1 cup flaked coconut

Directions
Cut apricots into small pieces with the kitchen scissors. Measure peanut butter and honey into a bowl. Mix thoroughly. Stir in chopped apricots. Drop by teaspoon into flaked coconut and roll until coated. Shape into balls, put on waxed paper and chill in refrigerator until firm. Yield: 12 to 15 balls.

Note: The best preparation we can give children is confidence in themselves as thinkers. Dr. Marjorie Fields in her book Literacy Begins at Birth (Tucson: Fisher Books, 1989) believes that thinking is the key to real learning. (pp. 36 - 37)

245

Pineapple Pasta

Ingredients
12 ounces(350g) fettucine or egg
    noodles
1/4 cup natural peanut butter
4 tablespoons milk
1 tablespoon salt
1/4 cup crushed pineapple, drained

Directions
Bring water to boil in a large pot. Cream the peanut butter, milk,
salt, and pineapple in a bowl. Boil the noodles and stir gently.
Cook uncovered for 8 minutes. Drain. Add the noodles to the
peanut butter mixture. Stir until the noodles are covered. Yum!
Yield: 6 servings.

*Game: Instead of putting dinner on your child's plate, try putting a
treasure map there that will lead them to their dinner.*

246

Peanut Butter Wedgies

Ingredients
Celery
Carrots
Apples
Bananas
Any other favorite food
Natural peanut butter

Directions
Prepare foods by cutting, cleaning etc. Leave peanut butter out at room temperature. Spread peanut butter in between slices of same and different fruit and vegetables. Arrange on plate. If slices won't stick together, use toothpicks.

Activity: *Go on a picnic and when you are done with the picnic, make a waterslide out of the plastic tablecloth. Run a hose on it and slide!*

247

Poultry and Fish

Chicken, Chicken, I've been thinkin'
Nows the time to scurry
Run before you're in the pot
With dumplings, rice, and curry

Honey Lover's Chicken

To "Sandpapery" *needs to be more of a batter!*

oh brother!

Ingredients

4 whole boneless chicken breasts
1/2 cup melted butter or margarine
2 tablespoons flour
2 tablespoons prepared mustard
1/2 cup cornflake crumbs
1/2 cup yellow cornmeal
1 teaspoon salt
1/4 teaspoon paprika

Directions

Preheat the oven to 350°F (180°C). Remove the skin from the chicken breast. Cut each boneless breast in half lengthwise. Blend flour and mustard into melted butter until smooth. Dip chicken pieces in butter mixture and coat well with crumbs and seasonings. Place on a shallow foil-lined pan and drip remaining butter mixture on top. Bake 35-40 minutes or until tender. Dip into honey and eat. Can also be refrigerated and taken for lunch. Yield: 4 servings.

248

very good 4/94

Chicken Puff

Ingredients
1 1/2 cups unbleached flour
2 teaspoons baking powder
1/4 teaspoon salt
2 eggs, separated
1 cup milk
2 cups cooked chicken
2 teaspoons onion, grated *2-3 scallions*
1/2 cup grated carrot *(or leftover veggies)*
2 tablespoons butter, melted
1 cup chicken gravy *or cream of chicken soup*

Directions
Preheat oven to 425°F (220°C). Mix flour, baking powder, and salt in a bowl. Stir in beaten egg yolks and milk. Add chopped chicken, onion, carrot, and melted butter. Blend well. Beat egg whites until stiff and fold into chicken mixture. Pour into greased casserole dish. Bake about 25 minutes or until lightly browned. Serve with hot chicken gravy and crisp green vegetables. Yield: 4 servings.

Note:
Here is my youngest son's favorite chicken joke...
Why did the chicken cross the road softly?
Because he was only a little chicken and he couldn't walk hardly!

249

Tortilla Chicken Nest

Ingredients

3 cups chopped cooked chicken
1 1/2 cups grated sharp cheese
1/4 cup chopped parsley or chilies
1/2 cup sandwich spread

1 tablespoon chopped onion
1/2 teaspoon cumin
1 tomato, sliced
1 1/2 cups tortilla chips

Directions

Combine chicken, 1 cup cheese, chilies, sandwich spread, onions, and cumin. Mix lightly. Spoon the mixture into a 11/2 quart casserole. Bake at 350 °F (180°C) for 25 minutes or microwave for 6 to 8 minutes, stirring after 4 minutes. Remove from oven and top with tomatoes. Arrange chips around edge of the casserole. Continue baking another 10 minutes or 2 to 3 minutes in the microwave. Serve with rice and a finely shredded lettuce salad. Yield: 4 - 6 servings.

Note: *Some children like green chilies and others don't. We've suggested parsley as a substitute. It will be tasty, but not spicy.*

250

Happy Chicken Curry

Ingredients

3 tablespoons butter or margarine
1 small onion, chopped
1 clove garlic, quartered
3 tablespoons flour
1 tablespoon ginger

1/2 teaspoon salt
2 tablespoons curry powder
1/2 cup coconut milk
2 cups milk
1 cup chicken broth or bouillon
3 cups cooked chicken, diced

Directions

Melt the butter and add the onion and garlic. Simmer for 5 minutes. Remove garlic and stir in the flour, ginger, salt, and curry powder. Combine the coconut milk, milk, and broth. Gradually add to the flour mixture and stir constantly over a low heat. When thickened and smooth stir in the cooked chicken. Heat through, but do not boil.
Serve with fluffy rice or chapattis. Yield: 6 servings.

Note: *Coconut milk in this recipe is the kind extracted from grated fresh coconut - not the watery liquid found inside a mature coconut.*

251

Chicken Biscuit Casserole

Ingredients

2 cups cooked chicken or turkey
3 tablespoons butter or margarine
1/2 cup onions, thinly sliced
1/2 cup celery, chopped
1/2 cup carrots, chopped
3 tablespoons flour
1/2 cup frozen peas
3 cups chicken broth or stock

Dumplings

1 cup unbleached flour
2 teaspoons baking powder
Pinch salt
1 egg, beaten in 1/3 cup milk

Directions

Preheat oven to 400°F (200°C). Cut chicken into cubes. Melt the butter in a frying pan and lightly saute the onions, celery, and carrots. Sprinkle the flour over the vegetables and blend into the juices. Gradually add the broth and stir as mixture thickens. Add the peas and season with salt and pepper. Pour the mixture into a greased casserole dish. Prepare the dumplings by sifting the dry ingredients into a bowl and quickly stirring in the egg mixture. Add additional flour to make a stiff dough. Divide the dough and shape into 8 balls. Drop the dough balls onto the casserole and bake uncovered 15 minutes or until biscuits are cooked through. Yield: 8 servings

252

Creamy Chicken Enchiladas

Ingredients

16 ounces (500g) plain yogurt or sour cream
1 can (250g) cream of mushroom soup
1/4 ounce (250g) can diced green chilies
1/4 teaspoon cayenne pepper
16 corn tortillas
2 cups cooked chicken, shredded
16 slivers of cheddar cheese
1 medium onion diced

Directions

Preheat oven to 350°F (180°C). Mix together yogurt, soup, chilies, cayenne, and salt to taste. Spread 1/2 of the mixture on the bottom of an 13 x 9 inch pyrex dish. Down the center of each tortilla, place a tablespoon of chicken, a sliver of cheese and a teaspoon of onion. Roll up and place side by side in pyrex dish. Pour remaining soup mix over enchiladas. Top with grated cheese if desired. Bake for 20 minutes or until enchiladas are heated through. Yield: 8 servings.

253

Chicken Niblets and Hula Sauce

Ingredients

1/4 cup vegetable oil
4 - 6 boneless chicken breasts
1 egg
1/4 cup unbleached flour
1 cup plain breadcrumbs

Sauce:

Melt together 1 cup grated cheese
1/4 cup pineapple juice, 1 tablespoon
honey, and 1/2 teaspoon
curry powder.

Directions

Preheat oven to 450°F (230°C). Pour 2 table-spoons of oil onto a cookie sheet and coat surface. Cut chicken into 1 1/2 inch chunks. Beat egg with 2 tablespoons oil. Arrange 3 flat bowls - one for flour, one for egg and one for breadcrumbs. Coat chicken first with flour, then egg and finally bread-crumbs. Arrange on cookie sheet, turning to coat with oil. Bake 15 minutes or until lightly browned. Dip in sauce.

((knock))
knock

254

Chicken Broccoli Quiche

Ingredients

1/2 pound(500g) broccoli, rinsed
3 eggs
1 cup milk
1/4 teaspoon ground nutmeg
1/4 teaspoon ground pepper
1 cup chopped cold cooked chicken
1 cup shredded cheese
1 partially baked 9-inch pie shell

Directions

Preheat oven to 350°F (180°C). Thinly slice broccoli stalks and cut flowerets into small pieces. Steam (or microwave) broccoli until tender. about 5 minutes. Let cool. Beat eggs, milk, nutmeg, and ?gether. Spread broccoli, chicken, and cheese evenly in ?our egg mixture over the top. Bake until fairly firm, ?inutes. Center will jiggle when gently shaken. Cool 15 ?fore serving. Yield: 6 servings.

255

Chicken Lips and Dips

Ingredients
4 chicken breasts, boned and skinned
1 cup flour
1/4 teaspoon paprika
1/2 teaspoon salt
3 tablespoons vegetable oil
1 cup buttermilk

Directions
Slice chicken into strips. Combine and sift together all the dry ingredients. Dip chicken in buttermilk then roll in seasoned flour. Heat oil in a skillet and cook the chicken uncovered about 10 minutes on each side, turning once. Drain on absorbent paper. Yield: 4 servings.

Dips
1. Tomato ketchup
2. Warm red jelly
3. Barbeque sauce
4. Teriyaki sauce

256

Turkey Turnovers

Ingredients

2 9″ unbaked pie crusts
2 cups cooked turkey meat, chopped or ground
1 cup mixed vegetables, canned or frozen
1/2 cup turkey gravy
1 egg, beaten

Directions

Preheat oven to 375°F (190°C). Remove pie crusts from containers and press into flat circles. Spread one half of each pastry circle with 1/2 the turkey meat, vegetables, and gravy. Fold over and seal edges with some of the beaten egg. Place turnovers on a greased cookie tray and brush with remaining egg. Bake for 25 minutes or until shiny brown. Serve with whipped potatoes and creamed corn. Yield: 6 servings.

Note: It's a good idea to always have bread on the table because children will generally eat bread if nothing else pleases them. Other flour products such as tortillas, rolls, or bagels will do just as well.

257

Sweet and Sour Fish

Ingredients

1 small can pineapple
1 package frozen fish sticks
1 tablespoon soy sauce
2 tablespoons vinegar

1 teaspoon ground ginger
2 tablespoons brown sugar
2 tablespoons cornstarch

Directions

Drain pineapple and reserve juice. Add water to juice to make 2 cups of liquid. Cut fish sticks into thirds. In a saucepan place liquid, soy sauce, vinegar, ginger, brown sugar, and pineapple. Bring to a boil. Mix cornstarch to a smooth paste with a little water. Add to mixture while stirring constantly. Bring to a boil. Simmer for 5 minutes then add fish pieces. Gently heat through. Serve over fluffy white rice. Yield: 4 servings.

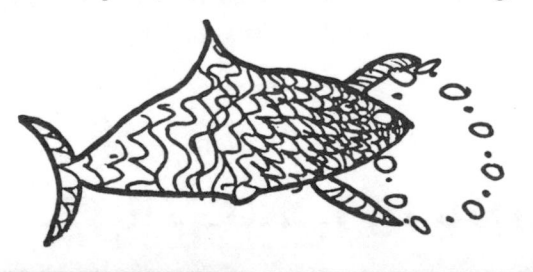

258

Scampi for Scamps

Ingredients

1/2 pound (250g) of medium shrimp
1/2 cup butter or margarine
1 tablespoon olive oil
2 teaspoons parsley flakes
1/2 teaspoon basil flakes
1/4 teaspoon oregano
1/4 teaspoon garlic powder
1/4 teaspoon salt
1 teaspoon fresh lemon juice

Directions

Preheat oven to 450°F (230°C). Peel and devein the shrimp, leaving tail on. Split each shrimp down the inside lengthwise. Spread open to look like butterflies and then place in a shallow baking dish. Melt butter and add remaining ingredients. Pour over shrimp. Bake for only 5 minutes then place under the broiler for 5 minutes or until shrimp have flecks of brown. Serve with fluffy rice and steamed vegetables. Yield: 4 servings.

259

Salmon Croquettes

Ingredients

1 pound (500g) can salmon
1 cup mashed potatoes
1/2 cup cracker crumbs
1 teaspoon salt
1 beaten egg

1 tablespoon parsley, chopped
1 small onion, chopped
1 teaspoon Worcestershire sauce
1/4 cup vegetable oil

Directions

Drain and flake the salmon and then blend in the mashed potatoes. Add the remaining ingredients except the oil. Mix well and form mixture into small croquettes. Croquettes will be slightly sticky, so roll in 1/2 cup cracker crumbs until well-coated. Fry quickly in hot oil. Drain well on paper towels and serve while still warm. Yield: 8 - 10 croquettes.

Note: Make the croquettes in the morning and place in the refrigerator. The coating will adhere better after being chilled and your preparation time for dinner will be reduced.

260

Halibut with Lemon-lime Butter

Ingredients

1/2 teaspoon lemon zest
1/2 teaspoon lime zest
2 tablespoons butter
1 1/2 pounds (750g) halibut (boneless)

Directions

Stir lemon and lime zest into softened butter. Put the butter mixture on a piece of plastic wrap and roll to form a 1" cylinder. Put in refrigerator to firm while preparing fish. Put the fish in a microwave-proof dish with 1/2 cup water and then cover with plastic wrap. Poke several holes in the plastic and cook for 4 to 6 minutes. Turn dish half way through cooking time. Drain off water and place cooked fish on serving plate. Top each portion with 2 slices of lemon-lime butter and serve with rice and a vegetable. Yield: 4 servings.

Note: Herbed butters are delicious served with baked or steamed fish. Try adding finely chopped parsley or fresh herbs. If you have one, use a butter pat to shape into balls or ovals.

261

Creamed Shrimp on Toast

Ingredients
1 pound (500g) fresh or frozen shrimp
2 cans of cream of shrimp soup
1 cup grated cheese
Toast

Directions
Heat together in double boiler the soup and the cheese. Stir until well blended. Boil and shell the shrimp if it is fresh. Add the prepared shrimp to the soup mixture and heat through again. Meanwhile, make toast and cut into strips or bite-sized pieces. Pour the creamy shrimp over toast and serve. Yield: 8 servings.

Note: *Creamed shrimp is a good dish to have for a hot lunch and can be served with a salad or crisp fresh vegetables. Seasonings can be added according to taste. Also, my kids enjoyed this dish with crab meat or other chopped shellfish.*

262

Creamy Fettucine Fish

Ingredients
1 - 2 pounds of fresh or thawed fish filets
Parsley
White sauce
Fettucine noodles
Salt and pepper to taste

White Sauce
3 tablespoons butter or margarine
3 tablespoons unbleached flour
1/2 teaspoon salt
2 cups milk

Directions
Cut the fish filets into bite-size pieces and steam until done (or microwave in a glass dish). Meanwhile, prepare the white sauce. Gently heat butter with flour, mixing until smooth. Add salt and a shake of pepper. Gradually add milk while continuing to stir to avoid lumps. Allow to boil gently and briefly. Chop parsley. Add to sauce with fish pieces and keep warm. Cook fettucine. Serve creamy fish sauce over noodles and if desired, sprinkle parmesan cheese on top. Yield: 4 servings.

Note: When it comes to fish, I've found that children prefer white fish such as Orange Roughy, halibut, and sole. It is very important that all the bones are removed.

263

SALADS

Olives, peppers, spinach greens
can be mixed with kidney beans
tuna, crab or large size prawns
blended in with chopped pecans
bits of apple, bits of pear
toss it high into the air
use a platter or a mold
serve it warm or serve it cold
top it with a fresh squeezed lime
SUPER SALADS everytime!

Rice Salad

Ingredients

1 cup long-grain rice
Peanut or vegetable oil
1 tablespoon sugar
Pinch of dry mustard
2 tablespoons white wine vinegar
2 teaspoons poppy seeds
1 large navel orange, peeled and sectioned
8 ounces (225g) pineapple sections, drained
1/2 cup sliced strawberries

Directions

Cook rice following package directions. Transfer while still warm to a large bowl. Add 1 tablespoon of oil and toss lightly. Cool. In a bowl combine sugar, mustard, salt to taste, and vinegar. Beat until sugar has dissolved. Gradually beat or blend in 1/4 cup of oil. Add poppy seeds and pour over rice. Add orange, pineapple, and sliced strawberries. Toss lightly and serve. Yield: 4 servings.

264

German Hot Potato Salad

Ingredients

5 or 6 medium potatoes
4 slices bacon
1/4 cup finely chopped onion
1 tablespoon flour
1 teaspoon dry mustard
1 teaspoon salt
1 tablespoon sugar
1/2 cup water
1 egg
1/4 cup vinegar

Directions

Scrub potatoes, drop them into a pan of rapidly boiling water, enough to cover by about 2 inches. Cook until tender. Drain. Hold potatoes under running water and peel off skin. Slice immediately into 1/2" rounds. Cook bacon in a skillet until crisp. Drain, and chop into small pieces. Pour all but 2 tablespoons of bacon fat from skillet and stir in onion. Cook until golden brown. Blend in flour, mustard, salt, and sugar. When smooth, stir in water and cook, stirring, 1-2 minutes. Place egg in a bowl and beat until blended. Stir in 2 tablespoons of hot mixture, add remaining hot mixture and vinegar. Pour over still-hot potatoes. Sprinkle with bacon. Yield 8 to 10 servings.

265

Apple Tuna Salad

Ingredients

7   ounces (200g) water
    packed tuna, drained
1/2 cup sliced celery
1   cup diced unpared apple
1/4 cup natural plain yogurt
1/4 cup mayonnaise
1   tablespoon lemon juice
1-2 tablespoons honey
Salt and pepper to taste

Directions

Combine the tuna, celery and apple. In a separate small bowl, mix
yogurt with the mayonnaise, lemon juice, salt, pepper, and honey.
Toss with the tuna mixture and refrigerate. Spread on favorite
bread, crackers, or place on top of a lettuce salad.
Yield: 4 to 6 servings.

266

Mandi's Orange Salad

Ingredients

1/2 cup sliced almonds
3 tablespoons sugar
1/2 head iceberg lettuce
1/2 head romaine lettuce
1 cup chopped celery
2 green onions, sliced thin
1 11-ounce (315g) can
mandarin oranges, drained

Dressing

1/4 cup vegetable oil
2 tablespoons chopped parsley
2 tablespoons sugar
2 tablespoons vinegar
1/2 teaspoon salt

Directions

In a small pan, cook almonds and sugar, stirring until almonds are coated and sugar dissolved; set aside. Mix lettuce, celery, and onions; refrigerate. Mix dressing ingredients together and chill. Just before serving, add almonds and oranges to lettuce. Toss with the dressing. Serve. Yield: 6 servings.

267

Fruity Fall Salad

Ingredients

3-ounce (74g) packet lime jello
1/2 cup mayonnaise
2 tablespoons lemon juice
1/4 teaspoon salt

1 cup chopped apples
3/4 cup seedless grapes
2 kiwi fruits, peeled and sliced

Directions

Dissolve the jello in 1 cup of hot water. Add 1/2 cup of cold water, mayonnaise, lemon juice, and salt. Blend well with a rotary beater or electric mixer. Pour into a freezer tray and quick chill for about 15 minutes. Turn chilled mixture into a bowl and beat again for about 3 minutes. Fold in the fruit. Mold. Yield: 4 servings.

Note: *This salad can be set in a fancy mold or in a pyrex dish. Before serving, briefly sit in hot water and then invert salad onto a serving dish. You and your child can gather Fall leaves together and arrange them around the serving dish for a seasonal appearance.*

268

Cashew Chicken Surprise

Ingredients

8 ounces (450g) uncooked shell macaroni
5 cups cubed, cooked chicken
1 cup diced celery
8 ounces (450g) sweet peas, thawed
1 cup prepared buttermilk dressing RANCH
1/2 cup whole cashews (omit if child is under 3 years)
Lettuce leaves

Directions

Cook pasta to desired doneness as directed on package. Drain and rinse. Place pasta, chicken, celery, and peas in a medium size bowl. Pour ranch dressing on top and stir. Refrigerate until serving time then sprinkle cashews on top and decorate with lettuce leaves. Yield: 6 to 8 servings.

269

Tuna Flowers

Ingredients

1 cup tuna packed in water, drained
1/2 cup diced celery
2 tablespoons lemon juice
1/4 cup light mayonnaise
2 avocados, halved
2 tomatoes, sliced and peeled

Directions

Put tuna, celery, lemon juice, and mayonnaise in a bowl and mix.
Take seed out of avocado and place tuna salad in the center of
avocado. Place tomato slices around the avocado like flower
petals. If it is spring, go outside and collect real flowers to
decorate plate. (Do not eat flowers.) Yield: 4 servings.

270

Perfect Potato Salad

Ingredients

5 medium potatoes
4 hard-boiled eggs, cooked
   and peeled
1 teaspoon salt
1 teaspoon sugar
1/2 teaspoon pepper
1 teaspoon prepared mustard
1/2 cup sweet pickles, chopped
1/4 cup bell pepper, chopped
1 cup light or safflower mayonnaise

Directions

Cook potatoes in salted water until they feel tender. Refrigerate until cool. Peel potatoes and cut into bite-size chunks. Cut eggs in half putting egg yolks in a small bowl. Cut the egg whites and put them in with the potatoes. Add mayonnaise to the egg yolks and mix until smooth. Add all other ingredients to bowl of potatoes. pouring mayonnaise mixture over the top. Mix gently and well. Refrigerate. Yield: 8 to 12 servings.

271

Asparagus Egg and Company

Ingredients

2 cups well-drained cooked asparagus cut
   into pieces
3 sliced hard-cooked eggs
1 head of lettuce
1/2 cup natural plain yogurt
2 teaspoons chopped chives
2 tablespoons lemon juice
1 teaspoon salt

Directions

Put egg and asparagus in dish and chill. Break lettuce up into small
pieces, wash, drain,.and chill. When ready to serve, mix yogurt,
chives, lemon juice, and salt. Pour over the egg and asparagus.
Put on top of the lettuce salad and eat! Yield: 4 to 6 servings.

272

I Spy Spinach Salad

Ingredients

2   bunches spinach, cleaned, drained, and torn
1   head letttuce, torn
2   hard-cooked eggs, chopped
4   tablespoons real bacon bits
6   mushrooms, sliced

Dressing

1/2 cup honey
1/2 cup lime juice

Directions

Place first 5 ingredients in a bowl and toss. Combine honey and lime juice in a small saucepan and heat until warmed. Pour over spinach salad and serve immediately. Yield: 6 servings.

Activity: Start a vegetable garden for your child. You will be amazed—they will start to enjoy eating their vegetables!

273

Jenny's Fruit Jello

Ingredients

22 ounces (550g) mandarin oranges, drained
20 ounces (500g) crushed pineapple, drained
3 ounces (85g) orange jello
Small carton of cottage cheese
Small carton of non-dairy whipped topping

Directions

Put the oranges and the pineapple into a bowl. Sprinkle the dry orange jello on top and stir gently. Add cottage cheese and whipped topping. Stir until mixed together. Chill in the refrigerator before serving. Yield: 6 servings.

Question: Ask your child what his or her favorite food is; then tell them what you used to eat and like when you were a child.

274

Orange and Chicken Salad

Ingredients

6 cups torn lettuce
11-ounces (312g) mandarin
   orange segments, drained
1/2 cup sliced green pepper
1/2 cup diced celery
1 cup diced, cooked chicken
   or turkey
Mayonnaise
Orange juice

Directions

Chill salad greens. Combine remaining ingredients and chill
separately. When ready to serve, combine and toss together
lightly with mayonnaise thinned with a bit of orange juice.
Yield: 6 servings.

275

Wild Rice Salad

Ingredients

4   ounces (110g) wild rice
2   tablespoons pineapple juice
3   slices fresh pineapple, cored and
     diced, or 8-ounce (225g) can pineapple
     tidbits, drained
1/2 cup diced celery
2   medium-size tart, crisp apples,
     cored and chopped
3/4 cup chopped walnuts
3/4 cup light or safflower mayonnaise

Directions

Cook wild rice according to package directions. Drain and transfer
to a large bowl. Stir in pineapple juice. Add pineapple, celery,
apples, walnuts, and mayonnaise. Toss to combine ingredients.
Chill and serve. Yield 4 servings.

276

Matchstick Salad

Ingredients

3 slices whole-grain bread
4 tablespoons butter, melted
1 clove garlic
1/2 pound (250g) cooked ham
2 carrots, peeled
1 head romaine lettuce

4 hard-cooked eggs
1 cup cherry tomatoes
Favorite salad dressing
Parmesan cheese

Directions

Brush both sides of bread with butter. Toast in 350°F (180°C) oven for about 5 minutes on each side. Cut garlic in half and rub over both sides. Cut toast into 1/2 inch croutons. Cut ham, and carrots into matchsticks. Tear lettuce into pieces and put into salad bowl. Top with quartered eggs, ham, carrots, cherry tomatoes, and croutons. Toss with salt, pepper, and salad dressing. Sprinkle with parmesan cheese and serve.

Note: A simple oil and vinegar dressing works best, but we have found that our kids prefer a creamier dressing. So we keep a good supply (made with buttermilk and a packet mix) on hand.

277

Snow Crab Salad

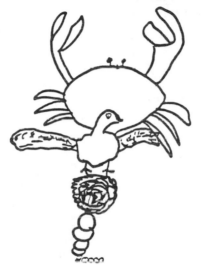

Ingredients
Fresh lettuce
8 ounces (225g) snow crab
Favorite dressing
Tomatoes
2 hard-boiled eggs
4 ounces (110g) frozen peas

Directions
Rinse and tear lettuce leaves into small pieces. Cut tomatoes,
into wedges. Peel and slice eggs. Toss lettuce, crab, tomatoes
and peas together. Pour dressing over salad and toss once more.
Serve with French bread. Yield: 4 to servings.

278

Crunchy Potato And Carrot Salad

Ingredients
1 cup shredded carrots
1/2 cup light or safflower mayonnaise
1 cup diced celery
2 chicken breasts cooked, skinned,
   boned, and diced
1 can shoestring potatoes

Directions
In a medium bowl, mix together carrots, mayonnaise, celery, and chicken. Cover and chill until ready to use (at least 2 hours). Top with potatoes. Yield: 4 servings.

Note: *Some children are finicky eaters. A very stubborn child may choose not to eat for several meals or even several days, but she should be served her meals with the family and her plate shoud be removed when the rest of the family have finished. In* <u>*The Practical Parent*</u> *by Painter and Corsini, (Simon & Schuster: New York, 1984), p. 56.*

279

Ring Around Of Jello

Ingredients

1   envelope unflavored gelatin
2   tablespoons honey or sugar
1 1/2 cups apple or orange juice
1 1/2 cups grated carrots
8   ounces (225g) crushed pineapple
1   tablespoon lemon juice

Directions

In medium bowl, mix gelatin with sugar. Heat 1/2 cup of the juice
to boiling; add to the gelatin and stir until gelatin is completely
dissolved. Stir in the remaining ingredients. Pour into a 1-quart
round mold (or shallow square dish) and chill until firm.
Yield: 6 servings.

*Activity: Save the leafy end of the carrots and start a "Veggie
Jungle." Put the carrot cut end down in a shallow tray and wait for
new leaves to sprout.*

280

SANDWICHES

Mary had a little ham
a little bread, a little jam
a little mayo, little cheese
stuck between two little leaves
looked peculiar, tasted great
that little sandwich Mary ate.

Giant Cooked Sandwiches

Ingredients

8 slices white bread
Butter for spreading
8 slices cheddar cheese
4 slices ham
4 eggs
1 teaspoon salt
1/2 teaspoon mustard
1 1/2 cups milk

Directions

Preheat oven to 350°F (180°C). Spread bread lightly with butter.
Sandwich together, with one slice of ham and cheese in each
sandwich. Place in a greased 9-inch square pan and top with
remaining slices of cheese. Whisk together eggs, salt, mustard
and milk. Pour over sandwiches. Bake for 35-45 minutes until
custard is set and cheese starts to brown. Serve warm. Try
adding other ingredients to your sandwich, kids love to participate
in this.   Yield: 4 to 6 servings.

281

Honeymoon Sandwich

Ingredients
Slices of bread, any kind
Lettuce
Mayonnaise
Salad dressing

Directions
Spread bread with salad dressing or mayonnaise. Layer on 2 or 3 lettuce leaves. Cover with another slice of bread. Trim crusts if desired. Yield: Varies.

Note: *Guidelines for children's table manners were first published in 1530. Erasmus of the Netherlands, wrote about the importance of instilling manners at an early age. "If you cannot swallow a piece of food," he wrote, "turn round discreetly and throw it somewhere."*

282

Fruity Bagel Sandwich

Ingredients
2 bagels, split and toasted
3 ounces (100g) cream cheese, softened
1 peach, thinly sliced
1 banana, thinly sliced
1/4 cup lemon juice
4 slices honeydew melon
1/4 teaspoon cinnamon

Directions
Spread the bagels with cream cheese and sprinkle with cinnamon.
Dip the peach and banana slices in lemon juice. Layer the fruit on
the bagels and serve with the melon. Yield: 4 servings.

Note: *Plain, egg, wholegrain or raisin bagels are best in this
recipe. Bagels, by the way, are very low in fat and liked by most
kids. The miniature ones are easy to handle and taste just as well.*

283

BLT Sandwich

Ingredients

4 slices toasted whole-grain bread
4 lettuce leaves, rinsed
1 large ripe tomato
4 strips lean bacon, cooked
1 tablespoon natural mayonnaise

Directions

Spread mayonnaise on each slice of toast. Cover 2 slices with lettuce, sliced tomatoes, and 2 strips of bacon. Place toast on top, cut each sandwich diagonally, and secure each triangle with a toothpick. Yield: 4.

Note: *Chores are an important part of a child's life and should not be a cause of parent-child conflict. Children need not be rewarded for doing a job. However, compliments and happiness are important. Chores are an expected part of the child's contribution to the family unit and can provide the base upon which responsibility and high self-esteem are built.*

284

Mighty Monte Cristo

Ingredients

12 slices white bread
Mayonnaise
12 slices Swiss cheese
6 slices cooked ham
6 slices turkey
3 eggs
1/4 cup half and half
  or milk
5 tablespoons margarine
Powdered sugar and jelly

Directions

Thinly spread one side of each bread with mayonnaise. Assemble 6 sandwiches, using 2 slices cheese and one slice each of ham and turkey. Trim bread crusts and filling with a sharp knife, making edges of sandwiches even. Cut in half diagonally. Beat eggs and half-and-half with a dash of salt. Place sandwiches in mixture and turn to coat. Let stand until all liquid is absorbed. Melt 3 tablespoons butter in frying pan over medium heat. Add sandwiches as will fit; cook, turning once, until lightly browned on both sides. Place sandwiches on an ungreased baking sheet and bake in a 400°F (200°C) oven until the cheese is melted (3 to 5 minutes). Dust with powdered sugar and serve hot with jelly. Yield: 6 sandwiches.

285

Raisinut Sandwich

Ingredients

1/2 cup peanut butter
1/2 cup cream cheese
1 tablespoon honey
1/4 cup raisins
1 tablespoon orange juice

Directions

Blend the peanut butter and cream cheese together. Add honey, raisins, and orange juice. Mix well. Spread on whole-wheat or raisin bread slices and serve open-faced with a glass of milk or natural apple juice. Yield: 8 servings.

Note: The sandwich was invented in England in the 1700's after the Earl of Sandwich who wanted to keep playing cards while he ate.

286

Egg Salad Sandwich

Ingredients
2 hard-boiled eggs
2 tablespoons natural mayonnaise
1/4 teaspoon dry mustard
1/4 teaspoon salt
Pepper to taste

Directions
Peel eggs and mash in a small bowl with a fork. Add mayonnaise, mustard salt, and pepper. Blend well. Serve between slices of cracked-wheat or other grain bread. Yield 4 sandwiches.

Note: In Jane Cooper's book, _Love at First Bite_ (1977), she suggests adding one or more of the following to the egg salad: pickle relish, crumbled bacon, toasted sunflower seeds, bean sprouts, grated carrot, chopped parsley, chopped celery, chopped chives, raisins, chopped ham, or fresh herbs such as basil and tarragon. _Love at First Bite_ is published by Alfred A. Knopf, NY.

287

Ploughmans Lunch

Ingredients

2 French bread rolls
4 thin slices of ham, beef or turkey
2 thick slices of Swiss cheese
1 ripe tomato, sliced
2 leaves of lettuce
Sweet pickled gherkins or onions

Directions

Split and spread rolls with butter or margarine.
Layer meat, cheese, tomato, and lettuce on
2 halves. Serve on a platter with sweet pickles
and coleslaw. Yield: 4 servings.

*Note: During preschool and kindergarten years, the correct
attitude about chores is built mostly by parent modeling and parents
<u>working</u> with the child. All children can be expected to clean up
messes they make, tidy their rooms, and make their beds.*

288

Seafood Sandwich

Ingredients

1 can tuna, water processed
1/2 cup sour cream
1 small onion, finely chopped
1/2 cup cucumber, peeled and chopped
1 tablespoon lemon juice
1/4 teaspoon salt
1 tablsepoon sweet relish or pickles

Directions

Combine all ingredients together in a bowl and mash with fork until evenly blended. To serve, spread between bread slices of your choice. Yield: 4 to 6 servings.

Note: *If you want your child to become interested in learning, the best way is to lead them, not force or cajole them. At the table talk about interesting subjects, such as science, books, history, the arts, and age appropriate current events.*

289

Banana and Honey Sandwich

Ingredients
Slices of whole-wheat or whole-grain bread
Natural honey, whipped or plain
Ripened bananas

Directions
Spread slices of bread with honey. Either place banana slices on top of honey or mash banana and spread on bread. Top with another slice of bread or eat as an open faced sandwich. These sandwiches can be cut into small pieces for younger children. Yield: Varies.

Note: *Bees may travel between 40,000 and 80,000 miles to make a pound (500g) of honey. Some fly as far as a mile from the hive to seek the nectar from which honey is made.*

290

Grilled Cheese Sandwiches

Ingredients

8 slices of wholewheat or wholegrain bread
2 tablespoons butter or margarine
4 slices of cheese, any kind

Directions

Preheat an electric or regular frying pan to medium heat. Butter one side of each slice of bread. Take 4 slices and place them buttered side down on the frying pan. Top each with a slice of cheese. Place the other slices of bread on top of cheese, buttered side up. Evenly brown the sandwiches and flip over to the other side. When brown on both sides remove and cut diagonally. Serve with a glass of milk or juice and slices of fresh fruit. Yield: 8 servings.

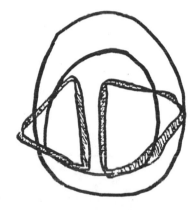

291

Sentence Sandwiches

Ingredients
Alphabet cereal
Sliced bread
Fruit jelly

Directions
Spread the slices of bread with fruit jelly (grape jelly or strawberry works well). Spread a handful of the cereal on a plate and then select appropriate letters to form words and simple sentences. Apply these to the bread slices. Serve as afterschool or Saturday snacks. Yield: Varies.

Note: *My children especially liked it when their name was spelled out on the bread and the message said "Welcome home" or "I love you" or "Feed the cat please."*

292

Goliath Sandwich

Ingredients
1 long loaf of French bread
Mustard and mayonnaise
1/4 pound (125g) thin sliced chicken
1/4 pound (125g) bologne
1/4 pound (1259) sliced cheese

Directions
Slice the bread horizontally in half, but not all the way through. Gently open the bread and lay it flat, but not separated. Spread mustard and mayonnaise on both sides and then layer on the sliced meats and cheese. Close the loaf and partly slice into 2 inch portions. Serve the giant sandwich on a bread board or wrap in foil and take on a picnic. Yield: 6 servings.

Note: *Remember, if you are going on a picnic and its a warm day you should omit the mayonnaise. Mayonnaise has a very short life outside the refrigerator!*

293

Pinwheel Sandwiches

Ingredients
Bread (thin sliced is best)
Sandwich spreads, such as
- tuna salad
- egg salad
- cheese spread

Directions
Prepare the sandwich spreads - the more colorful the better. Cut the crusts off the slices of bread and roll the slices flat with a rolling pin. Spread 1 tablespoon of spread on the bread. Starting with one side, roll the bread up. Slice the roll into wheels and arrange on the child's plate. Garnish with parsley and carrot curls. Yield: Varies.

Note: *Pinwheel sandwiches can be made with other fillings including peanut butter and jelly, cinnamon sugar, apple butter, cheese spread, and jams.*

294

Kid's Steak Sandwiches

Ingredients

2 tablespoons butter or margarine
1 large onion, sliced
1 pound (500g) thin roast beef slices
1 8-ounce (250g) jar process cheese spread
6 medium French bread rolls, split

Directions

Saute or microwave onions in butter until tender. Add meat and heat thoroughly. Heat process cheese spread in saucepan over low heat or microwave 30 seconds. Fill rolls with warm meat and onions. Top with cheese spread. Serve with fresh fruit slices or cut up raw vegetables. Yield: 6 servings.

Note: *For small children, use dinner rolls instead of French bread rolls and cut the beef slices into bite-sized pieces before stirring into onions. Most children prefer thin-sliced, tender meats that don't take a long time to chew.*

295

Sprinkle Sandwiches

Ingredients
Sliced bread
Butter, margarine, or cream cheese
Sprinkles or cake decorations

Directions
Spread the bread with butter, margarine, or cream cheese. Lightly sprinkle with the cake decorations or colored sprinkles. Cut into triangles and serve. For parties or special occasions, the bread can be cut into shapes before decorating. These make colorful snacks at children's parties. Yield varies.

Note: I used to love these as a child, only back then my mother spread a thin layer of sweetened condensed milk on the bread before adding the sprinkles which, by the way, we use to call "hundreds and thousands."

296

Sick Days

Hear me cough and sneeze
ooooh my aching head
Cheeks all pink with fever
Today I'm staying in bed.

Warm and fuzzy slippers
Lunch served on a tray
Extra Love from Mother
No school for me today!

Chilled Farina with Fruit Sauce

Ingredients

1 cup cooked farina or fine milled cereal
1/2 cup sliced peaches, fresh or canned
1 teaspoon apricot preserves
1/4 teaspoon vanilla extract
1/4 teaspoon lemon juice
1 teaspoon sugar

Directions

Cook farina according to package directions. Spoon into custard cup or child's bowl, cover and refrigerate until chilled. Put 1/2 of the peach slices into the blender and process until smooth. Combine puree, apricot preserves, vanilla, lemon juice, and sugar in a small saucepan and heat about 5 minutes, stirring constantly. Remove from heat. Chop remaining peaches and add to fruit sauce. Unmold farina onto a plate and top with sauce. Yield: 1 serving.

Note: *For easier unmolding, rinse molds with water before filling.*

297

Apple Souffle

Ingredients
2 apples, peeled
1 egg white
2 tablespoons sugar
1 tablespoon lemon juice

Directions
Core the apples and bake until tender. Beat the egg white until stiff and add to the apple. Stir in the juice and sugar. Serve in a small bowl or glass.

Note: Collect a box of toys, games, and books for those times when your child is sick or bed-ridden. Include puzzles, picture books, old photos, finger puppets, and surprises.

298

Grandma's Chicken Soup

Ingredients

1 chicken, boned and cut up
6 cups water
1/2 onion, diced
1/2 cup carrots, diced
1 small bay leaf
2 peppercorns
2 whole cloves
1/2 cup celery, chopped
1 teaspoon salt
1 package noodles

Directions

In a large saucepan, boil all the ingredients except the noodles, for 2 hours. Keep covered and stir occasionally. When done, strain. Chill and remove the fat. Pour broth back into saucepan and add chopped up chicken meat and the noodles which have been broken into small pieces. Cook for another 15 minutes or until the noodles are soft. Serve with cornbread. Yield: 12 servings.

299

Blancmange

Ingredients
1/2 cup sugar
6 tablespoons cornstarch
Pinch salt
4 cups milk
2 eggs, beaten
1 teaspoon vanilla

Directions
Mix the sugar, cornstarch, and salt in the top of a double boiler. While stirring, gradually add the milk. Stir constantly until it thickens. Cook for another 10 minutes. Remove 1 cup of the thickened mixture and add to beaten eggs. Return it to the double boiler and cook 2 minutes. Do not let mixture boil. Remove from heat and when slightly cooled, add the vanilla. Yield: 6 servings.

Note: *Blancmange can be spooned into prepared molds and decorated with fruit, such as mandarin oranges. Remember to wet the mold first.*

300

Poached Eggs on Toast

Ingredients

2 eggs
2 slices of whole-wheat toast
Vegemite, optional

Directions

Heat 2 cups water in a shallow, small frying pan. When just below boiling, carefully break eggs into water. Cook on low heat until whites are set. Lift out of frying pan and slide onto toast onto which Vegemite has been thinly spread. Remove crusts from toast if desired. Yield: 2 servings.

301

Robot's Rice Pudding

Ingredients
2 eggs
2 cups milk
1 cup cooked rice
1/4 cup sugar
1/2 cup raisins

Directions
Preheat oven to 350°F (180°C). Beat the eggs and sugar together and then add the milk. Grease a baking dish. Spread rice on bottom of dish and then sprinkle raisins on top. Pour the milk mixture over the rice and raisins. Place dish in a shallow pan and add water to pan. Bake custard for 25 to 30 minutes over water. Custard is done when golden brown on top and firm in the middle. This pudding can be baked in individual custard cups or small pyrex bowls. Yield: 4 servings.

302

Royal Broccoli Souffle

Ingredients

2 cups broccoli flowerets, chopped
3 tablespoons margarine or butter
3 tablespoons flour
3/4 cup milk
1/4 teaspoon cayenne pepper, optional

3 eggs, separated
1 teaspoon dry mustard
2 tablespoons parmesan cheese
Salt and pepper to taste.
1/4 teaspoon cream of tartar

Directions

Preheat oven to 400°F (200°C). Cook broccoli, drain, and mash. In a saucepan melt the butter and stir in the flour until smooth. Gradually add the milk and cayenne pepper. Cook over low heat until thick and smooth, stirring constantly. Remove from heat and add the beaten egg yolks. Whisk until blended. Add the broccoli, mustard, cheese, and salt and pepper.

Beat the egg whites until stiff and stir in cream of tartar. Fold 1/3 of the egg whites into the broccoli mixture and stir until blended. Fold in the remaining egg whites. Pour into a greased souffle dish or small ramekins and bake for 30 minutes. Bake ramekins for only 15 minutes. Serve immediately since souffle will lose its lightness and collapse if left to stand too long. Yield: 6 servings.

303

Cheese Soup

Ingredients

1/4 cup butter or margarine
1/4 cup unbleached flour
1 1/2 cups milk
Pinch of salt
1 cup grated cheese

1/4 cup onion, finely chopped
1/4 cup carrots, finely chopped
1/4 cup celery, finely chopped
2 cups chicken broth or bouillon
1 tablespoon chopped parsley

Directions

Melt butter in a saucepan or microwave and blend in flour.
Gradually add milk and salt. Cook, stirring constantly, until
thickened. Add grated cheese and stir until melted. Meanwhile,
parboil vegetables in chicken broth. Add to cheese mixture. Bring to
a simmer, but do not boil. Ladle into bowls and sprinkle with
parsley. Serve with plain zweiback or toast strips. Yield: 6 servings.

Note: On sick days children need lots of TLC, rest, and liquids.
Soups, juices, and glasses of water should be available between
meals.

304

Bavarian Cream

Ingredients
1 cup whole milk
1 package unflavored gelatin
2 eggs, separated
1/3 cup sugar
1/2 teaspoon vanilla extract
1/2 cup whipping cream
Maraschino cherries

Directions
Combine 1/2 the milk and gelatin in a small saucepan and let stand 5 minutes. Add remaining milk and stir over low heat until gelatin dissolves. Beat the egg yolks and sugar together in a medium bowl. Add vanilla and pour into the heated milk. Stir. Refrigerate until slightly set. Beat egg whites until stiff and beat the cream until stiff. Fold egg whites and whipped cream into gelatin mixture. Pour into a mold. Refrigerate until set. To serve, turn out onto a serving plate and top with cherries. In Bavaria this dessert is called *Bayerische Creme*. Yield: 6 servings.

305

Lemon Zweiback Bread

Ingredients

1 pound loaf of frozen bread
1 1/4 cups confectioner's sugar
1/4 cup lemon juice

Directions

Prepare and bake bread according to directions on packet. While bread is baking, prepare lemon glaze. Mix confectioner's sugar with lemon juice and stir until smooth. When the bread is cool, cut into 1/2 inch slices. Spread glaze over bread slices. Bake on a cookie sheet in a warm oven (250°F - 120°C°) for 30 minutes or until dry and crisp. Yield: 40 servings.

Note: Zweiback, also known as rusks or twice-baked bread, is very popular with children of all ages - especially teething babies. Older children like to spread plain zweiback with peanut butter or dip it in hot soups.

306

Ballerina's Bread Pudding

Ingredients
1/4 cup butter or margarine
6 slices of whole-wheat bread
1/2 cup raisins
4 cups milk
1/2 cup sugar
2 eggs
1 teaspoon vanilla extract

Directions
Preheat oven to 350°F (180°C). Spread the softened butter on the bread and if desired, trim off the crusts. Cut the slices into quarters and place face down in a baking dish, making 2 or 3 layers. Sprinkle the raisins over and between the bread. Beat the milk, eggs, sugar, and vanilla together. Pour over the bread. Place the dish in a shallow pan of water in the oven. Bake for 20 to 30 minutes or until the top is golden brown and the center is set. Cool slightly before serving. Yield: 6 servings.

307

Mellow Jello

Ingredients
1 package jello, any flavor
1 cup boiling waer
1 cup scalded milk or evaporated milk

Directions
Dissolve jello crystals in 1 cup boiling water. Let cool slightly. Stir in scalded milk. Some curdling may occur, but it wont affect the taste. Yield: 4 servings.

Variations
1. Add 1 small can crushed pineapple, drained, to Jello before it sets.
2. When slightly thickened, blend in a small container of lowfat cottage cheese
3. Instead of milk use a cup of fruit nectar, such as apricot.
4. Fold in a cup of miniature marshmallows
5. When almost set, cover with banana slices
6. Swirl in 1/2 cup of plain or vanilla yogurt.

308

Rosehip Syrup

Ingredients
2 cups fresh ripe rosehips
4 cups water
1/3 cup honey
1/2 cup fruit juice

Directions
Crush the rosehips in an enamel bowl and empty into a saucepan.
Cover with the water. Bring to a boil, then simmer covered for
about 45 minutes. Strain through a fine sieve or 2 layers of
cheesecloth. Add enough of the fruit juice to make about 4 cups
liquid. Warm the honey and stir into the syrup. Serve chilled.
Yield: 6 servings.

Note: *Rosehips are the fruits of rose bushes and are a wonderful
source of vitamin C. Wait to collect the rosehips until after the first
frost and they will be sweeter. Do not use hips if they have been
sprayed with fungicides or insecticides.*

309

Spanish Cream

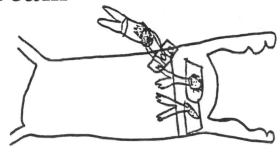

Ingredients
1 tablespoon plain gelatin
2 cups milk
4 tablespoons sugar
2 eggs, separated
1 teaspoon vanilla extract

Directions
Soften gelatin in a saucepan with a little milk. Add remaining milk and stir over a low heat until gelatin is dissolved. Add the sugar and beaten egg yolks. Stir with a wooden spoon until mixture thickens and coats spoon. Do not boil. Cool and add vanilla. Beat the egg whites until stiff. Fold into milk mixture. Pour into a wet mold and leave in fridge until set. Yield: 6 servings.

Note: *This dessert feels particularly cool and soothing on kids' sore throats. If made in a clear glass bowl, Spanish Cream has a pretty layered look.*

310

Lemon Barley Water

Ingredients
3 lemons
2 ounces (60g) sugar
3 ounces (90g) pearl barley
6 cups water

Directions
Peel the lemons very thinly. Place the peel in a large pitcher with the sugar and barley. Heat the water to boiling and pour over the barley and lemon. Let stand for 4 hours. Meanwhile squeeze the juice from the lemons. Strain barley mixture and add the lemon juice. Refrigerate until ready for use. Yield: 6 servings.

311

Baked Egg Custard

Ingredients
3 eggs
1/2 cup sugar
2 cups milk
1 teaspoon vanilla extract
1/4 teaspoon nutmeg, ground

Directions
Preheat oven to 325°F (160°C). Beat the eggs and then add the sugar, milk, and vanilla. Pour into a greased baking dish or a partially baked pie crust. Sprinkle top with nutmeg. Bake uncovered 30 minutes or until firm. If not using a pie crust, place baking dish in a shallow pan of water. Filling can be cooked separately and poured into baked pie shell when cooled. Yield: 4 - 6 servings

Note: *The color of eggs is determined soley by the breed of the chicken. Brown eggs are no more or less nutritious than white eggs - they are simply produced by a different breed of chicken.*

312

Fresh Fruit Ice Pops

Ingredients

2 cups fresh or frozen fruit juice
- orange
- apple
- pineapple
- grape
- mango

Coatings

Shredded coconut, crushed peanuts,
cookie crumbs, finely grated chocolate,
melted chocolate, jello crystals, and sprinkles.

Directions

Pour juice into ice-cube trays or popsicle molds. Leave overnight
or 4 hours until frozen. Dip tips in coatings. If inserting popsicle
sticks, wait until juice is almost hard so that sticks will stay upright.
Yield: 6 - 12.

313

Snacks

On a cracker or a chip
In a spread or with a dip
After breakfast, after lunch
all my snacks must have a... "CRUNCH!!!"

Cheese Pretzels

Ingredients

1 cup flour
2 tablespoons grated parmesan cheese
1/2 teaspoon salt
1/2 cup butter or margarine
1 cup shredded sharp cheddar cheese
2 to 3 tablespoons cold water

Directions

Preheat oven to 425°F (215°C). In a large bowl, stir together flour, Parmesan cheese, and salt. Using a pastry blender or 2 knives, cut in butter until mixture resembles fine crumbs. Stir in Cheddar cheese. Sprinkle water over flour mixture, 1 tablespoon at a time, stirring lightly with a fork until dough holds together. Shape dough into a ball, cut in half, cutting each half into 12 parts. Place each piece of dough on a lightly floured surface; roll back and forth with palms to make a strand. Shape into designs. Bake 12 minutes.

314

Egg Balls

Ingredients

6 eggs, hard-cooked and peeled
1 tablespoon mayonnaise
1 tablespoon soft margarine
1 tablespoon natural plain yogurt
1 teaspoon parmesan cheese
1 teaspoon Worcestershire sauce

Directions

Cut eggs in half lengthwise and remove yolks. Mash the yolks well; then stir in remaining ingredients (excluding egg whites) until smooth. Spoon back into one egg halve, putting other half on top to make a ball. Yield: 3 servings.

Note: *To tell if an egg is raw or hard-boiled, spin it on a table. If it wobbles and barely spins, it is raw. A hard-boiled egg will spin fast and easily.*

315

Puff Pastry Cheese Twists

Ingredients

8 ounces (225g) packaged puff pastry
1 egg
3/4 cup grated parmesan cheese

Directions

Preheat oven to 400°F (200°C). Roll out pastry 1/4 inch thick on a lightly floured surface to a neat square. Using a sharp knife, cut into strips 5 inches by 1/2 inch. Brush the strips with beaten egg and sprinkle with cheese, covering pastry evenly. Twist each pastry strip to form a spiral. Place on greased cooky sheet and bake for 7 to 10 minutes or until golden. Good lunch box snack! Yield: 12 to 15 servings.

Note: *Good eating habits can be easily learned when meals are planned to give a balanced diet and children are allowed to eat what they wish from what is placed before them. This is good advice from therapists Genevieve Painter and Raymond Corsine in* <u>The Practical Parent</u> *(New York: Simon & Schuster, 1984), p. 59.*

316

Toothpick Tidbits

Ingredients
Cheese cubes
Pineapple chunks
Carrot slices
Celery sticks
Cherry tomatoes
Prunes
Apple wedges
Ham cubes

Directions
Prepare the ingredients for eating. Arrange in small bowls or on a serving platter. Place toothpicks in a holder in the center. Have the children pierce 1 or 2 of the ingredients of their choice with a toothpick and discover a taste treat. Yield: Varies.

Note: Toothpicks are very dangerous in the hands and mouths of very young children. Keep them out of reach!

317

Nacho Popcorn

Ingredients
1/4 cup butter or margarine, melted
1/2 teaspoon paprika
1/2 teaspoon cumin
1/4 teaspoon red pepper
10 cups popcorn
1/2 cup parmesan cheese

Directions
Add the spices to the melted butter and stir until blended. Toss the popcorn in a large bowl with the butter mixture and the parmesan cheese until well-blended. Store in an airtight container. Yield: 12 servings.

Note: Corn popping is at least 5,000 years old and was originally perfected by the American Indians who cultivated 3 kinds of corn: sweet corn for eating, field corn for cattle feed, and so-called Indian corn for popping.

318

Cheese Puffballs

Ingredients
1/4 pound (125g) cheese, grated
3 tablespoons butter, softened
3/4 cup unbleached flour
1/2 teaspoon baking powder
1/4 teaspoon salt

Directions
Preheat oven to 425°F (220°C). Blend cheese and butter into dry ingredients. Mix into a stiff dough (add cold water if too dry). Form into small balls and place on a greased baking tray. Bake for about 12 minutes or until golden brown. Yield: 12 - 18 balls.

Note: This pastry can be used to make cheese straws and cheese twists.After mixing put dough in a pastry tube to make straws. To make twists, roll dough out thin, cut into narrow strips and twist.

319

Pocket Bread Pizza

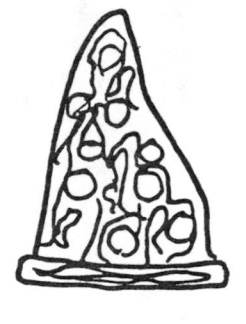

Ingredients
2 whole wheat pita bread pockets
1/2 cup pizza sauce
3/4 cup shredded mozzarella cheese
1/4 cup green pepper, chopped
16 slices pepperoni or bologne

Directions
Preheat oven to 400°F (200°C). With a sharp knife carefully separate pockets into thin rounds. Spread 2 tablespoons sauce on each half. Cover with a handful of cheese, 1/4 of the green pepper, and 4 slices of meat. Place on a cookie sheet and bake 10 minutes or until cheese is melted. Cool slightly and cut into quarters. Serve with milk and apple slices. This is a great afterschool snack. Yield: 16 servings.

Note: Children who grow up with unconditional love have high self-esteem and are more likely to be successful, contributing, happy members of society. For more about self-esteem, read Dorothy Corkille Briggs' book, Your Child's Self Esteem (New York: Doubleday, 1975)

320

Creamed Spinach Crescents

Ingredients

10-ounce (275g) package chopped spinach, thawed
1 cup shredded cheese
1/4 cup dry breadcrumbs
2 8-ounce (225g) cans refrigerated crescent rolls.

Directions

Preheat oven to 375°F (190°C). Squeeze the water out of the spinach. Combine the drained spinach, cheese, and breadcrumbs in a 1 1/2 quart saucepan and cook until cheese is completely melted, stirring often. Unroll dough and separate into 16 triangles. Cut each in half lengthwise forming 32 triangles. Spread each triangle with 1 teaspoon of mixture. Roll up starting at widest side. Place on greased cookie sheet and bake 10 to 13 minutes or until golden brown. Cool slightly before serving. (Filling can be prepared in the microwave oven.)

Yield: 32 snacks.

Note: *Did you know that a child will eventually eat approximately 5,000 pounds of food in a lifetime? That is equivalent to the combined weight of 4 or 5 elephants!*

321

Apple Cheese Wedglets

Ingredients
2 apples
1/4 pound (125g) cheese

Directions
Core apples and slice into 8 wedges. Cut cheese into 16 slices about same size as apple wedges. Place a slice of cheese on each piece of apple and arrange in shapes on child's place. Serve with a glass of cold milk.
Yield: 16 snacks.

Note: An apple a day will keep the doctor **and** the dentist away!

322

New Zealand Pikelets

Ingredients
10 ounces (275g) unbleached flour
2 teaspoons baking powder
2 tablespoons sugar
1 egg
1/2 cup milk
1 tablespoon melted butter

Directions
Preheat an electric frying pan or griddle to medium-high heat. Sift together the dry ingredients. Beat together the egg and the milk and pour into the center of the flour mixture along with the melted butter. Stir until blended. Drop spoonfuls onto the greased frying pan surface. When bubbles appear, flip over and brown other side. Cool on wire rack then serve with butter and jam. Yield: 24 pikelets.

323

Nifty Nachos

Ingredients
1 can nacho cheese soup or dip
1/4 cup of milk
8-ounce bag of tortilla chips
Chopped green onions
Chopped tomato

Directions
Heat the cheese sauce and stir in the milk. Preferably, use a glass measuring cup and microwave for 2 - 3 minutes covered. Let cool for a few minutes. Place the tortilla chips in small bowls and pour over the nacho sauce. Top with chopped green onions and tomato. This is a great finger food. Yield: 6 - 8 servings.

Note: Potato chips can be used instead of tortilla chips and I have also tried it with small crackers, such as wheat thins. It is always a good idea to keep cans of cheese soup on hand when cooking for children.

324

Crispy Cheese Critters

Ingredients
1 packet flour tortillas (10)
1 cup grated cheese
1/2 cup bacon bits

Directions
You will need a variety of animal-shaped cookie cutters for this snack. Cut out animal shapes from tortillas and place on a cookie tray. Spread the grated cheese in the center of each critter and then sprinkle the bacon bits on top. Place cookie tray under the broiler for 3 to 5 minutes or until the cheese bubbles. Allow cheese to cool a bit before serving. Make plenty because you will be surprised how quickly they disappear! Yield: 24 critters.

325

Date Pinwheels

Ingredients

8 ounces (250g) pitted dates
1 cup sugar
1 cup margarine
2 cups brown sugar
3 eggs

4 cups unbleached flour
1/2 teaspoon baking soda
1/4 teaspoon salt
1/2 teaspoon cinnamon

Directions

Cook the dates with sugar and 1 cup cold water over a low heat until thick, about 10 minutes. Beat margarine until light and add brown sugar. Blend well. Beat in the eggs. Sift together the dry ingredients and add to the creamy margarine mixture to form dough. Chill dough thoroughly and then divide into 4 parts. Roll each part into a rectangle 1/2 inch thick. Spread each rectangle with date mixture. Roll up like a jelly roll. Chill (overnight if possible). Cut with sharp knife into slices 1/2 inch thick. Bake on greased cookie sheet for 10 to 12 minutes at 400°F (200°C). Cool on rack. Yield: 24 -36 cookies.

326

Asparagus Rolls

Ingredients
Slices of brown bread
Butter, softened
Asparagus spears, cooked and drained

Directions
Thinly spread butter on slices of bread. Trim off the crusts.
Place an asparagus spear along one edge of the bread.
Roll up. Place seam side down on a cutting board. Repeat
with rest of bread and asparagus. Cut each roll into 3 small
ones and arrange on a plate with a sprig of parsley as the
garnish. Yield: Varies.

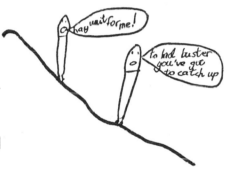

Note: *Asparagus is a very old plant which belongs to the lily
family. It has a bushy fern-like appearance when mature, but is
best known and widely cultivated for its tender, edible young
shoots called asparagus spears.*

327

Watermelon Rind Pickles

Ingredients

1 pound (500g) of watermelon rind
3/4 cup vinegar
3/4 cup water
1/2 cup sugar
1 teaspoon mixed whole pickling spices

Directions

Cut the watermelon rind into 1 inch pieces. Cook in boiling water for 10 minutes. Drain. Combine remaining ingredients and simmer for 3 minutes. Pack the rind in hot sterilized jars to 7/8 full. Pour over the pickling liquid. Seal and process 15 minutes in a boiling water bath Cool before storing. Chill before serving. These are colorful and tasty snacks. Yield: Varies.

Note: *In her book* <u>*Your Child's Self Esteem*</u>*, Dorothy Corkille Briggs states that helping children build self-esteem is the key to successful parenthood (p. 6). This is an excellent book published by Doubleday in New York (1975).*

328

Toasted Pumpkin Seeds

Ingredients

1 cup fresh pumpkin seeds
1 - 2 tablespoons butter, melted
Seasoned salt to taste

Directions

Preheat oven to 325°F (160°C). Rinse
pumpkin seeds and pat dry. Spread
seeds on a cookie tray. Drizzle with the
butter and sprinkle with salt. Bake for 1
to 1 1/2 hours or until brown, turning
often.

*Note: Be certain to use seeds from pumpkins which have not
been treated with fungicides or insecticides.*

329

English Peanut Brittle

Ingredients
1 cup sugar
1/2 cup light corn syrup
1 3/4 cups peanuts, dry roasted and unsalted
1 tablespoon butter or margarine
1 teaspoon vanilla extract
1 teaspoon baking soda.

Directions
Grease a baking sheet. In a large glass bowl, combine sugar and corn syrup. Cook 6 minutes in the microwave. Stir in peanuts with a wooden spoon. Cook another 6 minutes or until a small amount becomes brittle in cold water. Remove from microwave and stir in butter and vanilla. Blend in baking soda and stir until mixture is light and foamy. Pour onto prepared baking sheet and spread quickly. As candy cools, it can be stretched into a thin sheet using buttered hands. Cool completely then break into pieces and store in an airtight container. Yield: Varies

Note: *Peanuts are not nuts at all; they are legumes like peas and beans. Do not serve whole peanuts to children under 3 years.*

330

Soups

Tomato, potato, split pea or rice
Black bean and barley with pinches of spice
Broths of onion, chowders of clam
Noodles with chicken, turkey or lamb
Delicious aromas so steamy and hot
come from the soups you create in u pot!

Evalesi's Egg Rice Soup

Ingredients
3 cups chicken broth
2 egg yolks
1 can evaporated milk
1 cup white or brown rice, cooked
1/2 teaspoon salt
Pepper to taste

Directions
In a saucepan, heat chicken broth. Beat egg yolks and milk together. Pour 1/2 cup of broth into egg mixture, then pour the egg mixture in a thin stream into the broth in the saucepan. Heat gently until soup thickens slightly, stirring frequently. Add rice and season with salt and pepper. Serve hot with pretzel sticks or whole-wheat croutons. Yield: 4 servings.

Note: Dr's Genevieve Painter and Raymond Corsini believe that eating should be the child's business ... the less parents worry about eating, the better for everyone (p. 56). Their book, _The Practical Parent_, is well-worth reading. (New York: Simon & Schuster, 1984)

331

Cowboys Corn Chowder

very good 1/96
I also added fish 1 pound

Ingredients

3 tablespoons butter or margarine
1 clove garlic, minced
2 large onions, chopped
4 cups regular-strength chicken broth
1/2 teaspoon thyme leaves
1 bay leaf

1 pound thin-skinned potatoes
1 pound (450 g) frozen
  whole-kernel corn, thawed
2 cups milk
1/2 cup whipping cream
1 1/2 cups shredded sharp cheddar
  cheese
Crackers (optional)
Salt and pepper

Directions

Melt butter In a 6-quart pan over medium heat. Add garlic and
onions; cook stirring, until onions are soft. Stir in broth, thyme, and
bay leaf; bring to a boil. Cut potatoes into 1/2" cubes. Add to
boiling broth; reduce heat, cover, and simmer until potatoes are
tender. Stir in the corn, milk, and cream. Stir over low heat; do
not let soup boil. Season to taste with salt and pepper. Put
cheese in a bowl to pass at the table. Kids love to sprinkle cheese
and float crackers on top. Yield: 8 servings.

332

Tomato Rice Super Soup

Ingredients

3-4 cloves garlic, minced
1 tablespoon oil
5-6 tomatoes, peeled and coarsely chopped
2 quarts (2 liters) vegetable stock
3/4 cup cooked brown rice
1 teaspoon dill or thyme

Directions

Saute the garlic in oil, stirring constantly until golden. Add the remaining ingredients and simmer 10-15 minutes. Great on cold winter days! Yield: 8 servings.

Note: Every child should decide for himself how much, if any, he is to eat of the foods that have been prepared for him, state Genevieve Painter and Raymond Corsini in their book *The Practical Parent* (New York: Simon & Schuster, 1984), p. 56. He should be allowed to serve himself from serving dishes, they add.

333

Split Pea Swirl Soup

Ingredients
1 cup green split peas
2 quarts water
1/2 cup tomato sauce
1 onion, chopped
2 stalks celery, chopped
2 carrots, chopped
1/2 teaspoon oregano
Salt and pepper to taste.
2 tablespoons sour cream

Directions
Wash and soak peas for an hour before cooking. Drain and put in a large saucepan. Add water and bring to a boil. Skim top. Simmer, covered, for another hour. Add remaining ingredients except sour cream. Simmer 1 more hour. Ladle into soup bowls. Place a teaspoon of sour cream in center and using a knife, swirl. Serve with bagel chips or crusty French bread. Yield: 6 - 8 servings.

334

Matzo Ball Soup

Ingredients

6 cups chicken or beef stock
2 eggs, separated
3 tablespoons butter or margarine
3/4 cup matzo meal or cracker meal
1/2 teaspoon salt
1/8 teaspoon ginger or nutmeg
1 tablespoon parsley, finely chopped

Directions

Pour the stock into a large saucepan. Beat the egg yolks and softened butter in a medium bowl until thick. Pour 1/2 cup of hot stock over the egg mixture and blend well. Gradually add the dry ingredients and parsley, stirring constantly. Beat the egg whites until stiff, but not dry. Fold the egg whites into the matzo mixture and set aside (refrigerate if possible). About 30 minutes before serving soup heat stock to boiling and reduce to simmer. Shape dough into small balls and drop them into simmering broth. Cook covered for about 15 minutes. Yield: 6 servings.

335

Shrimp Bisque

Ingredients

2 tablespoons unbleached flour
2 tablespoons butter or margarine
3 cups skim milk
1/4 cup onion, finely chopped
1/4 cup celery, finely chopped
Salt and pepper to taste
1/4 teaspoon paprika
1 pound (500g) cooked baby shrimp

Directions

Blend butter and flour in a saucepan or microwave. Gradually stir in milk and heat until thickened. Cook onion and celery until tender. Drain and add to sauce. Stir in salt, pepper, and paprika. Simmer, stirring often, for 5 minutes. Fold in shrimp and heat through. Serve with crackers, unsalted pretzels or "goldfish" crackers. Yield: 4 servings.

336

Fresh Tomato Soup

Ingredients

2 tablespoons butter or margarine
1 onion, chopped
3 ripe tomatoes, peeled and chopped
3 tablespoons tomato paste
2 tablespoons unbleached flour
2 cups chicken broth
Salt and pepper to taste
1 cup half and half

Directions

Melt butter in small saucepan and add onion. Saute for 3 minutes. Stir in tomatoes and tomato paste. Cook for 3 minutes. Sprinkle with the flour and mix well with a wooden spoon. Add the broth, salt, and pepper stirring constantly. Simmer 15 minutes. Remove from heat and pour into a blender. Blend at high speed for 1 minute. Return to saucepan and add the milk. Heat through and simmer for another 2 minutes. Garnish with sprigs of parsely and serve with whole-wheat croutons. Yield: 4 servings.

337

Finnegan's Fish Chowder

Ingredients

1 tablespoon butter or margarine
2 scallions, sliced
1 carrot, sliced or grated
1 potato, peeled and diced
1/2 teaspoon salt

1/8 teaspoon pepper
1 bay leaf
1/2 cup water
1 1/2 cups milk
1/4 pound (125g) frozen fish

Directions

Melt butter in saucepan and saute scallions. Add carrot, potato, salt, pepper, bay leaf, and water. Heat to boiling. Reduce heat and simmer, covered for 10 minutes or until vegetables are almost tender. Add milk and cubed frozen fish. Heat to simmering. Cover and cook for 5 minutes until fish is tender. Yield: 2 servings.

Note:. *Best fish for this recipe (and most kids like these) are filleted sole, haddock, Orange Roughy, cod, and halibut.*

338

Chunky Cream of Vegetable Soup

Ingredients

4 cups vegetables - cauliflower, potatoes, peas, broccoli, carrots, celery, green beans, etc.
2 tablespoons butter or margarine
2 tablespoons unbleached flour
2 cups milk
Salt, pepper, and nutmeg to taste

Directions

Chop vegetables into bite-sized pieces after rinsing thoroughly. Steam until cooked, but still firm. Place about 2/3 of the steamed vegetables in the blender and blend until pureed. In a large saucepan, melt butter and stir in flour. Gradually add the milk and stir until smooth and almost boiling. Add the pureed vegetables then fold in the remainder of the steamed vegetables. Stir until blended and heated through. Add salt and pepper to taste and finally sprinkle nutmeg on top. Serve with bread sticks. Yield 4 servings.

Note: Kids don't appreciate cooked, stringy celery. For this recipe, chop celery very finely and do not put in the blender to puree.

339

Diddle Diddle Dumpling Soup

Ingredients

4 cups chicken stock or bouillon
1 cup cooked chicken, chopped
1/2 cup carrots, chopped
1/2 cup celery, chopped
1/2 cup onion, chopped

Dumplings

1 cup unbleached flour
2 teaspoons baking powder
1/2 teaspoon salt
1 egg, beaten
1/3 cup milk

Directions

Prepare soup by adding vegetables and chicken to broth in a large saucepan. Bring to a boil then simmer for 15 minutes. Sift the flour, baking powder, and salt into a bowl. Mix together the egg and milk and add to the dry ingredients. Stir until blended. Drop tablespoons of the dough into the soup, dipping spoon into stock first. Cover tightly and steam for 10 minutes. Test with a toothpick for doneness. Yield: 4 servings.

Note: The secret to making light dumplings is to keep them steaming on top of the simmering soup. Use a glass lid to watch the dough swell.

340

Galaxy Gazpacho

Ingredients

4 cups fresh tomatoes, diced
1 cup green pepper, chopped
1/2 cup green onion, chopped
1 clove garlic, pressed
1 small can tomato paste
2 cups bouillon, beef or chicken

1/2 cup lemon juice
1 tablespoon vegetable oil
1 teaspoon paprika
1/2 cup parsley, chopped
1 teaspoon vegetable salt.
Pepper to taste

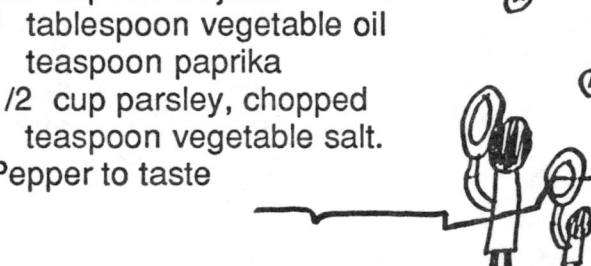

Directions

Place all ingredients in a food processor or blender in 2 batches. Blend until smooth and creamy. Pour into a serving bowl and chill for at least 3 hours. Serve with slices of cucumber and/or sour cream on top. Yield: 6 servings.

Note: An outrageous book for parents and kids to read is Delia Ephron's <u>How to Eat Like a Child</u> (Ballantine Books, 1978), in which she humorously describes lessons in not being a grown-up.

341

Creamed Potato Soup

Ingredients
2 large potatoes
2 stalks celery, chopped
1 onion, peeled and chopped
1/2 teaspoon salt
3 tablespoons butter or margarine
2 tablespoons flour
2 cups milk
Salt and pepper to taste
3 tablespoons chopped parsley

Directions
Peel and dice potatoes. Cook covered in 4 cups water with celery, onion, and salt until tender, about 20 minutes. Pour vegetables and water through food mill or blend in blender until pureed. Melt butter in pan or microwave. Stir in flour and mix well. Add flour paste to vegetable puree and blend in the milk. Reheat and season to taste. A few minutes before serving stir in parsley. Serve with breadsticks or toast strips. Yield: 4 servings.

342

Minestrone Soup

Ingredients

1 medium onion, chopped
1 stalk celery, diced
1 large carrot, sliced
3 tablespoons margarine
1 large potato
2 large tomatoes, peeled and cut

2 cans beef broth
1 teaspoon dry basil
1/2 cup uncooked macaroni
2 small zucchini, sliced
1 can kidney beans, drained
Salt and pepper

Directions

In a 5-quart saucepan over medium heat, cook onion, celery, and carrot in margarine, stirring constantly, until onion is soft but not browned. Add potato, tomatoes, broth, and basil. Bring to a boil. Reduce heat to a simmer. Cover and simmer for 15 minutes. Add macaroni and zucchini. Cook another 10 minutes. Add kidney beans and simmer until tender, about 5 minutes. Season to taste with salt and pepper. Pass parmesan cheese at the table to sprinkle on top. This soup is delicious and is a meal in itself. Yield: 6 servings.

343

Chunky Vegetable Soup

10

Ingredients

3 - 4 cups chicken broth
1/4 cup uncooked rice
2 carrots, diced
2 stalks celery, chopped
1 small zucchini, sliced

3 tablespoons margarine or butter
3 tablespoons flour
1 cup milk
2 tablespoons parsley, minced
Salt and pepper to taste

± chopped cooked chicken

Directions

Bring broth to a boil in a large saucepan. Add rice, cover, reduce heat, and simmer for 10 minutes. Add carrots, celery, and zucchini. Cover and simmer until vegetables are crisp tender, about 10 minutes. In a small saucepan, melt butter. Blend in flour and cook, stirring, until bubbly. Gradually pour in milk and then stir in 1 cup of the hot broth from soup. Cook until sauce boils and thickens. Stir sauce into soup, blending well. Add parsley and season to taste with salt and pepper. Cook until just heated through. Serve with wholewheat breadsticks or crusts of French bread. Yield: 6 servings.

344

Sunset Soup

Ingredients

1 leek (or use celery)
4 small or 2 large carrots
1 tablespoon butter or margarine
16-ounce (500g) can of tomatoes
1 cup tomato juice
1 teaspoon tomato paste
1/2 teaspoon thyme
2 cups chicken stock
Salt and pepper to taste

Directions

In a large saucepan, cook chopped leeks and carrots in butter. Stir in the tomatos, tomato juice, tomato paste, thyme, and chicken stock. Simmer covered for 30 minutes. Cool. Puree a cup at a time in the blender. Return to saucepan and reheat. Season with salt and pepper. Yield: 8 servings.

Note: This is a brightly colored soup which can be served with crusts of wheat bread brushed with melted butter and broiled.

345

Mulligatawny Soup

Ingredients

2 tablespoons butter or margarine
1 onion, peeled and chopped
1 apple, peeled, cored and chopped
2 teaspoons curry powder
1 tablespoon chutney

2 tablespoons flour
4 cups beef stock or bouillon
1 teaspoon lemon juice
1 teaspoon sugar
4 tablespoons rice
1/4 cup half and half milk

Directions

Melt butter and saute onion and apple. Add curry powder, chutney and flour. Blend well together. Gradually add stock, stirring constantly. Add lemon juce and sugar. Bring to a boil then simmer for 20 minutes. Strain the soup or puree in a blonder. Return to heat and add the rice. Gently boil for 12 minutes or until rice is tender. Add salt to taste and finally stir in the milk.
Yield: 4 servings.

346

Cauliflower Buttermilk Soup

Ingredients

1 ounce (25g) butter or margarine
1 large onion, peeled and chopped
1 clove garlic, peeled and crushed
1 tablespoon unbleached flour
3 cups milk
1 cauliflower, broken into florets
2 eggs, beaten
1 cup buttermilk
Salt, pepper, and nutmeg to taste

Directions

Melt butter in a saucepan and saute onion and garlic until golden.
Stir in the flour and cook, stirring for 1 minute. Gradually add the
milk, stirring constantly. Add cauliflower and simmer, covered, for
25 minutes or until cauliflower is soft. Puree the mixture in a
blender. Return puree to saucepan. Beat in the eggs, buttermilk,
and seasonings. Reheat gently and do not boil. Yield: 4 servings.

347

Vegetables

Brussel Sprouts and corn
Asparagus and beans
Radishes and cucumbers
Most type of greens

Turnips and cabbage
Spinach and tomatoes
Onions and mushrooms
Most kinds of potatoes

Squash, peppers and
espccially GREEN PEAS...
are just a few veggies
that cause me to sneeze!!!

Potato Pancakes

Ingredients

6 medium size potatoes
1 large onion
2 eggs
1/4 cup flour
1 teaspoon salt
pinch of sugar
3 tablespoons soured milk or cream
Applesauce

Directions

Grate potatoes and onion finely. Drain off any excess liquid and place in a mixing bowl. Add beaten eggs, flour, salt, sugar, and sour milk. Beat for 3 minutes. Drop mixture from a tablespoon into a frying pan of hot shallow fat and fry on either side until golden brown. Serve with applesauce.
Yield: 12 to 15 pancakes.

Note: To make sour milk, add one tablespoon of lemon juice to every one cup of milk.

348

Hot Diggity Bean Bake

Ingredients

15 ounces (425g) baked beans
2 tablespoons firmly packed
    brown sugar (optional)
2 tablespoons ketchup
1 1/3 cups buttermilk baking mix
1/2 cup shredded cheddar cheese
1/2 cup milk
4 turkey or tofu hot dogs

Directions

Preheat oven to 425°F (215°C). In a small saucepan; combine beans, sugar, and ketchup. Simmer uncovered, stirring occasionally until heated. Combine baking mix, cheese, and milk. Slice the hot dogs crosswise (not all the way through) Into 1/2" sections. Pour the beans into four baking dishes. Bend the hot dogs into a circle and put biscuit mixture into the center. Bake for 15 minutes. Yield: 4-6 servings.

349

Peas in White Sauce

Ingredients

1 package frozen peas
1 tablespoon butter or margarine
2 tablespoons flour
2 cups milk
Salt and pepper to taste

Directions

Cook the frozen peas according to directions on package or microwave until heated through. Drain. Make the white sauce by melting butter and stirring in the flour until mixture is smooth. Blend in 1/2 cup of the milk and heat, stirring constantly. Gradually add the rest of the milk and stir until mixture becomes thick and creamy. Heat until sauce just starts to boil. Add the cooked peas. Season with salt and pepper. Yield: 6 servings.

Note: Peas are a good source of protein as well as vitamins A and C.

350

Whipped Potatoes

Ingredients
6 Irish potatoes, medium size
2 tablespoons butter or margarine
Salt and pepper to taste
1/4 cup milk
2 tablespoons finely chopped parsley

Directions
Peel the potatoes and cut lengthwise. Place in a saucepan and just cover with water. Boil for 15 to 20 minutes or until tender. Drain well and leave with lid on for 3 minutes. Mash well with a potato masher until there are no lumps. Add the butter, salt, pepper, and milk. Whip with a fork or an electric beater until the potatoes are nice and fluffy. Stir in the parsley. Serve while still warm. Yield: 6 servings.

Note: *My middle son Andrew, likes to spread cold whipped potatoes on a slice of white bread or toast as a snack. He says it tastes delicious!*

351

Vegetable Frog Dip

Ingredients

Assorted raw vegetables
2 cups plain yogurt
1/4 cup chutney, chopped
1 teaspoon dried mint flakes, crumbled

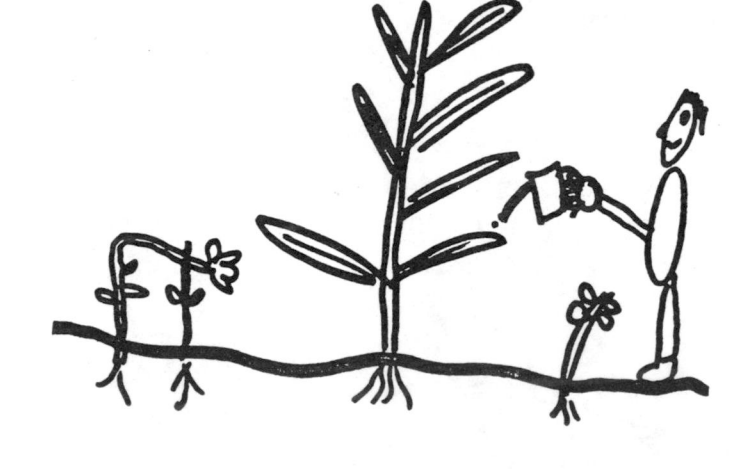

Directions

Rinse the vegetables and break or cut into bite-size pieces.
Arrange on a large platter. Mix together the yogurt, chutney and
mint. Stir until well-blended. Pour into a small bowl and place in
the center of the vegetables. Have ready as an afterschool snack.
Yield: 12 servings.

352

Corn and Carrot Pudding

Ingredients

3 tablespoons butter or margarine
2 onions, grated
3 tablespoons flour
1/2 teaspoon curry powder
1/2 teaspoon salt
1 cup milk
1 cup each cooked carrots and corn
1 cup breadcrumbs

Directions

Preheat the oven to 375°F (190°C). Melt 1 tablespoon of the butter and cook onion until soft. Add flour, curry, sugar, salt and lastly milk, stirring constantly. When sauce is smooth and thick, fold in carrots and corn. Pour into an oven proof dish. Melt remaining butter and brown breadcrumbs. Spread buttered breadcrumbs over top of vegetable mixture. Bake uncovered for 30 minutes. Serve warm with fish or chicken. Yield: 4 servings.

353

Scalloped Potatoes

Ingredients

4 medium potatoes
4 tablespoons butter
4 tablespoons flour
2 cups milk

1 cup grated cheese
Salt and pepper
1/4 teaspoon paprika

Directions

Peel and cook the potatoes then set aside to cool. Make 2 cups of cream sauce by melting the butter and blending in the flour. Heat gently and while stirring constantly, slowly add the milk. Keep stirring until the sauce begins to thicken. Add the grated cheese and salt and pepper to taste. Add the cut up potatoes and mix well together. Pour into a buttered casserole and sprinkle with paprika. Bake at 350°F (180°C) for about 10 minutes or until well heated through. Yield: 4 servings.

Note: *This cream sauce can be made quickly and easily in the microwave oven in a glass bowl. Other vegetables can be used instead of potatoes, for example cauliflower, peas, or broccoli.*

354

Vegetable Patties

Ingredients

1 beaten egg
1 grated carrot
1 finely chopped onion
1 peeled and grated potato

1 cup flour
1 teaspoon baking powder
Salt and pepper to taste
Cooking

Directions

Preheat a skillet or electric frying pan. Put all the vegetables in a bowl and stir in egg. Mix the dry ingredients together and add gradually to the vegetables. Batter should be moist and fairly thick. Pour 3 tablespoons of oil into the frying pan and wait until it gets hot. Drop spoonfuls of batter into the oil. Cook 5 minutes and turn over. Continue frying until golden brown. Test the first patties with a toothpick to make sure the insides are cooked through. Adjust the temperature and the cooking time to suit. Serve with Ketchup. Yield: 18 patties.

Note: *Dr Majorie Fields, author of <u>Literacy Begins at Birth</u> (Tucson: Fisher Books, 1989) says that the most important aspects of storytime are the cozy feelings of togetherness... these feelings become associated with books and lead to reading as an enjoyable pastime. (p. 104)*

355

Golden Roast Potatoes

Ingredients
4 medium potatoes
2 tablespoons butter or margarine
Salt and pepper to taste

Directions
Preheat oven to 350°F (180°C). Scrub the potatoes. Peel only if marred or where green. Cut into wedges or quarters. Melt butter and brush potatoes. Sprinkle a little salt and pepper over skins. Place potatoes in a greased small roasting pan. Bake for 20 to 30 minutes or until golden brown. Potatoes can also be roasted in an electric frying pan. Try surrounding a roasting chicken or turkey with the potatoes during the last 20 minutes of cooking. Yield: 6 - 8 servings.

356

Crinkly Coleslaw

Ingredients

1 1/2 pounds (375g) cabbage, curly kind
1/2 cup shredded carrot
3 tablespoons grated onion
1 teaspoon salt
1 teaspoon sugar
1/2 teaspoon celery seed (optional)
1/4 teaspoon pepper
2 tablespoons vinegar
3/4 cup mayonnaise

Directions

Finely shred cabbage and crisp in ice water for an hour or longer. Drain thoroughly. Add carrot and onion and toss. Mix together the remaining ingredients in a measuring cup. Pour over cabbage and toss once more. Add a handful of raisins if desired. Yield: 6 servings.

357

Frittata

Ingredients

2 eggs, beaten
1 baked potato, peeled and sliced
1/2 cup cooked broccoli or peas
1 tablespoon scallions, chopped
1 tablespoon pimento, chopped
1 tablespoon water
Salt and pepper
1 tablespoon vegetable oil
1 tablespoon parmesan cheese

Directions

Combine all the ingredients except oil and cheese in a bowl. Heat the oil in a frying pan with a flameproof or removable handle. Pour mixture into frying pan and cook until underside is browned. Season to taste with salt and pepper. Sprinkle cheese on top and broil until top is browned. Cut into squares or wedges and serve warm. Yield: 4 servings.

358

Turkey Topped Potatoes

Ingredients

2 teaspoons butter or margarine
1 tablespoon onion, minced
1/2 cup mushrooms, sliced
2 teaspoons unbleached flour
3/4 cup broth or water
Salt and pepper to taste
1/2 cup plain yogurt
1 cup cooked turkey, chopped
2 baked potatoes

Directions

Melt margarine in saucepan. Add onions and saute briefly. Add mushrooms and stir. Sprinkle flour over mixture and blend well. Gradually add broth, salt, and pepper, stirring constantly. Cook until thickened. Add turkey and yogurt and heat through. Do not boil. Split potatoes and break up insides a little. Spoon turkey mixture over each half and serve with soup and a salad. Yield: 4.

359

Corn Souffle

Ingredients

1/4 cup milk
1/2 cup grated cheddar cheese
1/2 cup mayonnaise
1/4 cup flour

Salt and pepper
1 cup corn
2 tablespoons chopped parsley
4 egg whites

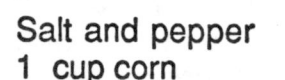

Directions

Preheat over to 325°F (160°C). Heat mik and cheese until cheese melts. Mix mayonnaise, flour, salt, and pepper in a small bowl. Slowly stir in the milk and cheese mixture, corn, and parsley. Beat egg whites until stiff in a large bowl. Gently fold corn mixture into egg whites. Pour or slide into greased 1 quart souffle dish. Bake uncovered for 50 minutes or until a silver knife comes out clean when it is inserted into center. Serve at once. Yield: 4 servings.

Souffle tips:

1. A souffle must be eaten when it is ready.
2. Do not try to double or halve the recipe.
3. Cool the sauce before adding the egg whites.
4. Beat egg whites until the are stiff and creamy; not hard and dry.

360

Bubble and Squeak

Ingredients
Leftover cooked vegetables
Cold mashed potatoes
Butter or margarine
Tomato ketchup

Directions
Melt butter or margarine in skillet or frypan. Chop up leftover vegetables and break up mashed potatoes. Add all vegetables to frying pan and flatten with a spatula. Cook at moderate heat for 10 minutes or until the underside is a golden brown. Flip the vegetables over with the spatula a small section at a time. Cook another 10 minutes. Put on plate and drizzle with tomato ketchup. Serve at breakfast instead of hash browns. Yield: Varies.

Note: *This recipe is a good one for usng up leftovers. The name "Bubble and Squeak" is from England, but the dish is cooked in Canada, Australia, and New Zealand as well.*

361

Broccoli Cheese Potato Boats

10+ 1/95

Ingredients
2 potatoes
11/2 cups cheese sauce
2 tablespoons sour cream
1/2 teaspoon mustard
1 cup cooked broccoli flowerets

Directions
Scrub potatoes and bake until cooked (1 hour in an oven or 8 - 10 minutes in the micro-wave). While potatoes are baking, stir together the cheese sauce, sour cream, and mustard until smooth. Gently heat in a saucepan or microwave for 2 - 3 minutes. Stir in the cooked broccoli flowerets and heat once more. Let the potatoes cool for 10 minutes and then split open. Soften the insides with a fork and place in the center of the child's plate. Spoon the sauce over the split baked potatoes and serve with tomato wedges or orange slices. Yield: 4 servings.

Note: Canned cheese sauce may be used instead of homemade sauce.

362

Hashbrown Heaven

Ingredients

1 pound (500g) frozen shredded potatoes
1 cup milk
1/4 cup butter or margarine
1/4 cup chopped parsley
1 tablespoon onion flakes
1/2 teaspoon salt
1/3 cup grated cheddar cheese

Directions

Thaw potatoes. Bring the milk to a boil and add potatoes. Cook until liquid is absorbed. Remove from heat and add butter, parsley, onion and salt. Stir. Transfer to a greased casserole dish. Sprinkle grated cheese on top. Bake uncovered, for 1 hour or until golden brown on top. Yield: 4 servings.

363

Cheesey Cottage Fries

Ingredients
24 frozen cottage potato fries
4 ounces (125g) sharp natural cheddar cheese
12 cherry tomatoes
Toothpicks

Directions
Place the frozen cottage fries on a cookie sheet and cook according to directions on package. Meanwhile slice the cheese and then cut into 24 1-inch squares. Cut the tomatoes in half. Remove cottage fries from oven and top each one with a cheese square and a tomato half. Secure with a toothpick. Return to oven for a few minutes until cheese is just melted. These snacks are best served warm. Yield: 24 snacks.

Note: *Instead of frozen cottage fries, try potato puffs. Flatten them slightly and use a bottle cap to cut round shapes in the cheese slices. The kids will enjoy helping you prepare these snacks.*

364

Peter Rabbit Pockets

Ingredients
1/2 cup plain yogurt
1/2 cup shredded zucchini
1/4 teaspoon dill weed
8 boiled ham slices
2 pita bread rounds
Tomato slices
4 slices of processed cheese
Lettuce
Radish slices
Salt and pepper to taste

Directions
Combine yogurt, zucchini, and dill weed. Mix well. Cut pita rounds
in half and spread inside of each with 2 tablespoons of mixture.
Roll up ham and fill bread with ham rolls, tomatoes, cheese,
lettuce, and radishes. Top with remaining yogurt mixture.
Yield: 4 servings.

365

I've now learned what nutrition means
it's saying "Goodbye" to jelly beans
goodbye to hidden candy jars
to drawers stuffed with chocolate bars
to donut holes, to sugar pops
to potato chips and lemon drops.
It's saying "hello" to raisins
mixed Granola in a bowl
to apples topped with cinnamon
fresh honey on a roll!

Conversion Table

Liquid or dry ingredients:

1/4 cup = 60 ml
1/3 cup = 80 ml
1/2 cup = 125 ml
3/4 cup = 190 ml
1 cup = 250 ml
2 cups = 500 ml

1/4 teaspoon = 1.5 ml
1/2 teaspoon = 3 ml
1 teaspoon = 5 ml
3 teaspoons = 15 ml
1 tablespoon = 15 ml

1 inch = 25 mm
1/2 inch = 12 mm
1/4 inch = 6 mm

Temperatures:

250°F = 120°C
275°F = 140°C
300°F = 150°C
350°F = 180°C
375°F = 190°C
400°F = 200°C
425°F = 220°C
450°F = 230°C

Weights:

1 ounce = 30 grams
4 ounces = 125 grams
8 ounces = 250 grams
16 ounces = 500 grams
2 pounds = 1 kilogram

Index

Breads

Apricot Carrot Loaf, 32
Best Banana Bread, 21
Bread Sticks,
Cinderella's Pumpkin Bread, 25
Easy No-Knead Wholewheat Bread,
Hansel and Gretel Gingerbread, 23
Lazy Daisy Loaf, 29
Lemon Zweiback Bread, 306
Leprechaun Soda Bread, 28
Magical Cinnamon Rolls, 17
Monkey Bread, 81
Oatmeal Raisin Bread, 27
Plump Pear Bread, 16
Zucchini Bread, 18

Breakfasts

Apple Cheese Omelet, 39
Applesauce Pancakes, 34
Aunt Katy's Coffee Cake, 44
Buttermilk Oat Cake, 38
Blueberries in the Wild, 47
Cinnamon Toast, 101
Designer Omelettes, 75
Dutch Roll-Ups, 45

Broccoli

Broccoli Cheese Potato Boats, 362
Broccoli Mushroom Lasagna, 221
Chicken Broccoli Quiche, 255
Royal Broccoli Souffle, 303

Eggs Bennie, 36
Fruit Surprise, 49
German Pancakes, 46
Gingerbread Pancakes, 42
Ham Cakes, 50
Holiday French Toast, 159
Hawaiian Toast, 37
Magical Cinnamon Rolls, 17
Carob French Toast, 33
Oatmeal Add-Ons, 68
Peanut Butter Granola, 243
Peanut Butter Oatmeal, 234
Peanutty Pancakes, 232
Pear Plumps, 35
Designer Pancakes, 67
Puff Baby, 48
Tomato Tunnels, 43
Yogurt Souffle, 41

Carrots

Apricot Carrot Loaf, 32
Carrot Raisin Muffins, 30
Corn and Carrot Pudding, 353
Crunchy Potato and Carrot Salad, 279

Cheese

Apple Cheese Omelet, 39
Apple Cheese Wedglets, 322
Cheese and Tomato Quiche, 190
Cheese Dumpling Soup, 104
Cheese Pretzels, 314
Cheese Puffballs, 319
Cheese Soup, 304
Cheesy Cottage Fries, 364
Cheddar Cheese Cookies, 182
Crispy Cheese Critters, 325
Grilled Cheese Sandwiches, 291
Homemade Cheese, 103
Macaroni and Cheese, 215
Mac and Cheese Omelet, 222
Macaroni Cheese Medley, 231
Potato Cheese Saucers, 187
Puff Pastry Cheese Twists, 316
Savory Cheese Muffins, 26

Chicken

Cashew Chicken Surprise, **269**
Chicken Biscuit Casserole, **252**
Chicken Broccoli Quiche, **255**
Chicken Dunkers, **235**
Chicken Fruit Pasta Salad, **220**
Chicken Lips and Dips, **256**
Chicken Niblets and Hula Sauce, **254**
Chicken Puff, **249**
Creamy Chicken Enchiladas, **253**
Fruit Flake Chicken, **111**
Grandma's Chicken Soup, **299**
Happy Chicken Curry, **251**
Honey Lover's Chicken, **248**
Italian Chicken Risotto, **129**
Orange and Chicken Salad, **275**
Oven Fried Chicken, **195**
Tortilla Chicken Nest, **250**

Cookies

ANZAC Fruit Bars, **138**
Butterscotch Faces, **56**
Cheddar Cheese Cookies, **182**
Cream Cheese Cookie Balls, **61**

Chewy Fruit Bars, **189**
Chocolate Pinwheels, **53**
Christmas Cookies, **16**
Date Pinwheels, **49**
Detective Cookies, **51**
Dream Bars, **57**
Chocolate Chippers, **62**
Fun Fortune Cookies, **66**
Gingerbread Giants, **58**
Ice Cream Cone Cakes, **202**
Kiwi Krisps, **120**
Lilly's Layered Bars, **115**
No Bake Apricot Drops, **245**
Miss Ginger Snap, **64**
Oatmeal Pan Cookies, **59**
Oatmeal Raspberry Bars, **52**
Peanut Apple Cookies, **233**
Peanut Kiss Cookies, **54**
Pie Crust Rolls, **65**
Pig's Tails, **79**
Pineapple Bars, **55**
Puppet Show Cookies, **60**
Rice Mallow Bars, **63**

Corn

Corn and Carrot Pudding, **353**
Corn Souffle, **360**
Corny Corn Muffins, **24**
Cowboy's Corn Chowder, **332**

Designer

Butterscotch Faces, **56**
Clubhouse Sandwiches, **77**
Collage Melt, **70**
Cracker Crunchies, **73**
Designer Omelettes, **75**
Egg Cups, **199**
Food Sculpture, **76**
Heavenly Star Pizza, **72**
Kid's Kebabs, **83**
Layered Vegetable Salad, **80**
Mashed Potato Sculpture, **74**
Monkey Bread, **81**
Oatmeal Add-Ons, **68**
Picture Pancakes, **67**
Pig's Tails, **79**
Tide's Out Sundaes, **78**
Tortilla Towers, **82**
Tropical Eggs, **69**

Foreign Foods

Bavarian Cream, **305**
Beef Sate and Silky Sauce, **127**
Chapattis, **123**
Cornish Pasties, **126**
Creamy Enchiladas,
Dim Sims, **124**
French Crepes Suzette, **116**
German Hot Potato Salad, **265**
German Pancakes, **46**
German Raisin Crepes, **118**
Italian Chicken Risotto, **129**
Katrina's Kasha, **128**
Kiwi Krisps, **120**
Latkes, **131**
Lemon Zweiback Bread, **306**
Leprechaun Soda Bread, **28**
Middle Eastern Lamb, **166**
Moroccan Couscous, **125**
Nasi Goreng, **117**
New Zealand Pikelets, **323**
Oriental Pork Stir-Fry, **122**
Pirate's Paella, **121**
Quesadillas, **130**
Scotch Eggs, **119**
Weiner Schnitzel, **181**

Fruit

4th of July Fruit Plate, **155**
ANZAC Fruit Bars, **138**
Apple Fritters, **133**
Apple Zinger, **10**
Apricot Sticks, **145**
Berries and Cream, **110**
Blueberries in the Wild, **47**
Bountiful Blueberry Pie, **97**
Candy Apples, **147**
Cantaloupe Canoes, **143**
Caramel Apple Chunks, **139**
Chocolate-Dipped Bananas, **140**
Cottage Cheese and Melon Slices, **146**
Cranana Crush, **1**
Cranberry Sherbert Delight, **134**
Cranberry Tea, **4**
Fairytale Ambrosia, **141**
Fall Fruit Medley, **136**
Fresh Fruit Ice Pops, **313**
Fruitin' Tootin' Dip, **209**
Fruit Pudding Nog, **5**
Fruit Salad Cake, **98**
Fruit Surprises, **49**
Fruit Tapioca, **92**
Fruity Bagel Sandwich, **284**
Fruity Banana Split, **132**

Fruity Fall Salad, **268**
Gooseberry Flan, **135**
Hot Apple Scrunch, **137**
Mr P.B. Blueberry, **238**
Peach Crumble, **90**
Pear Plumps, **35**
Pineapple Bars, **55**
Pineapple Wreath, **164**
Pot of Gold Salad, **144**
Raisin Surprise Baked Apples, **95**
Raspberry Clouds, **210**
Raspberry Tart, **93**
Red Hot Applesause Swirl, **142**
Strawberry Fizz, **9**
Strawberry Pie, **87**
Strawberry Pudding, **99**
Strawberry Shortcake, **96**
Tootie Fruitie Smoothie, **7**
Watermelon Rind Pickles, **328**
Watermelon Whirl, **2**
We 3 Fruit Slurpy, **148**
Yogurt Fruit Shake, **107**

Potatoes

Apple Potato Folds, **194**
Broccoli Cheese Potato Boats, **362**
Cheesy Cottage Fries, **364**
Creamed Potato Soup, **342**
Crunchy Potato and Carrot Salad, **279**
German Hot Potato Salad, **265**
Golden Roast Potatoes, **356**
Hashbrown Heaven, **363**
Latkes, **131**
Mashed Potato Sculpture, **74**
Perfect Potato Salad, **271**
Potato Cheese Saucers, **187**
Potato Pancakes, **348**
Scalloped Potatoes, **354**
Turkey Topped Potatoes, **359**
Whipped Potatoes, **351**

Pumpkin

Cinderella's Pumpkin Bread, **25**
Toasted Pumpkin Seeds, **329**

Rice

Crockpot Lamb with Wild Rice, **179**
Donna's Noodle Rice, **223**
Egg and Rice Soup, **331**
Italian Chicken Risotto, **129**
Nasi Goreng, **117**
Party Rice, **208**
Rice Mold, **230**
Rice Salad, **264**
Robot's Rice Pudding, **302**
Sweet Brown Rice Custard, **85**
Tomato Rice Super Soup, **333**
White Rice, **226**

Salads

Apple Tuna Salad, **266**
Asparagus Egg and Co., **272**
Cashew Chicken Suprise, **269**
Chicken Fruit Pasta Salad, **220**
Crunchy Potato and Carrot Salad, **279**
Rice Salad, **264**
Fruity Fall Salad, **268**
German Hot Potato Salad, **265**
I Spy Spinach Salad, **273**
Jenny's Fruit Jello, **274**
Layered Vegetable Salad, **80**
Mac Roni's Cold Salad, **229**

Mandi's Orange Salad, **267**
Matchstick Salad, **277**
Menorah Pineapple Salad, **160**
Orange and Chicken Salad, **275**
Perfect Potato Salad, **271**
Pot of Gold Salad, **144**
Ring Around of Jello, **280**
Snow Crab Salad, **278**
Wild Rice Salad, **276**
Rice Salad, **264**
Tuna Flowers, **270**

Turkey

Turkey Topped Potatoes, **359**
Turkey Turnovers, **257**

Veal

Veal Roll-Ups, **180**
Weiner Schnitzel, **181**

Vegetables

Broccoli Mushroom Lasagne, **221**
Bubble and Squeak, **361**
Cauliflower Buttermilk Soup, **347**
Cheesy Cottage Fries, **364**
Creamed Spinach Crescents, **321**
Chunky Creamy Vegetable Soup, **339**
Chunky Vegetable Soup, **344**
Corn Carrot Pudding, **353**
Corn Souffle, **360**
Crinkly Coleslaw, **357**
Frittata, **358**

Golden Roast Potatoes, **356**
Hashbrown Heaven, **363**
Hot Diggity Bean Bake, **349**
I Spy Spinach Salad, **273**
Layered Vegetable Salad, **80**
Peas in White Sauce, **350**
Peter Rabbit Pockets, **365**
Potato Pancakes, **348**
Royal Broccoli Souffle, **303**
Scalloped Potatoes, **354**
Turkey Topped Potatoes, **359**
Vegetable Dip, **201**
Vegetable Flat Bread, **186**
Vegetable Frog Dip, **352**
Vegetable Patties, **355**
Whipped Potatoes, **351**
Zucchini Bread, **19**

Yogurt

Applesauce Yogurt Ice, **88**
Yogurt Banana Shake, **14**
Yogurt Fruit Shake, **107**
Yogurt Souffle, **41**

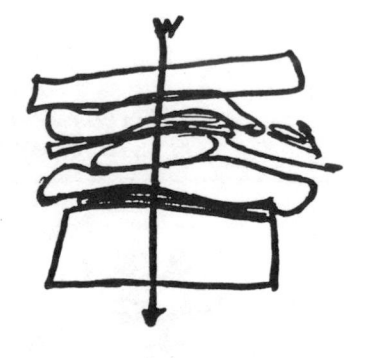

A special thanks to Ormandale School in Portola Valley, California. To the teachers: Earlyne Mund, Kathy Kobara, and Sue Stewart, and especially to the children who illustrated our recipes.

Jennifer Ann Vigh Upjohn!!!

Ian

Baldwin

Dane Holderman

Karen Twelves

Neal Ambron

Kelly Barrett

SARAH MINTZ!

Andrea Feeley!

mikiya Matsuda

Hayden Moulds!

ALison Dohrmann

David Sloan

Todd Hunt

Jeffrey Frey

Devon Wahsj

Daniel Silberman

Missy Woodrow

Dayeh

Suzanne

Luca

Jay Ritchey

Ali Rasch

Kristin

@MATT Skrobo

Joshua ☒ McLaren

James # Roblich

Sandy Ballentine

Sharon Terwilliger

Allison Wagner

Matt Sams

Sean Bieer

David Nelligan

Riley Bradley

Jessica Kornberg

joshua sternbach

Ryan Forster

Lucinda Lannie

Kelly Nichols

Daniel Mazawa

Micah Johnson

Julie Falconer

Justin Martin

tyler Bushnell

Julie Castello

Shane Sykes

Matt Kanzler

Lauren Rosenthal

Vanessa Salsbury

Ryan Piaget

Kate Parmer

Becky Latter

Stephanie Balogh

Jenny Bond

Margaret Word

Rachel Samuels

Peter Bergman

Rebecca sternbach

Ted Conrad!

Paul wagner

Nick cOnrad

NIRos Hunner

Amanda.O. Conradt

Trevor F. Crane

Morgan? Jackson.

Paul*Oikawa

Mike katz

Kimberly Nicky epprecht

Intersimone

Rachel Saal

Dr. Judith Gray is a teacher of Childrens Movement and a well know author of dance books and articles. She is a mother of four. A former executive director of the Girl's Club of Tucson, Judith is currently a school administrator for the San Mateo, CA school district.

Sheila Ellison has a degree in Child Psychology from the University of Southern California, and is a Certified Massage Therapist. The mother of four children, she has many talents and interests, including jewelry design and fabrication, painting, and sculpture.

From the authors and staff at Forward March we sincerely hope you have enjoyed our product and we look forward to serving you in the future.

If you would like to order additional copies of this book, or information on other titles published by Forward March™Press, such as "365 Days of Creative Play," or "365 Creative Party Ideas," just drop us a note or give us a call. We would be pleased to hear from you.

Contact us at: *Forward March™Press*
2701 Conestoga Dr., Suite 121
Carson City, NV 89706
(702) 885-8988